A Time for
Compassion

A call to cherish and protect life.

Dr. RON LEE DAVIS with
JAMES D. DENNEY

A Time for
Compassion

A call to cherish and protect life.

Dr. RON LEE DAVIS with
JAMES D. DENNEY

Fleming H. Revell Company
Old Tappan, New Jersey

Library of Congress Cataloging-in-Publication Data

Davis, Ron Lee.
  A time for compassion

  (A Crucial questions book)
  Includes bibliographies and index.
  1. Abortion—Religious aspects—Christianity.
2. Pro-life movement—United States.   I. Denney,
James D. II. Title.
HQ767.2.D38   1986   241'.6976   86-13955
ISBN 0-8007-1492-X

Contents

Publisher's Foreword

IN A WORLD THAT HAS BECOME AN INTERRELATED GLOBAL VIL-
LAGE of 4.5 billion men, women, and children, the problems
of human existence have reached crisis proportions. Modern man stretches to achieve new heights, but his very ad-
vances in technological and scientific realms sometimes
threaten him with the loss of life's most precious gifts—and
even life itself. In the midst of the crises, Christians believe
the possibility for unprecedented good, for the flourishing
of freedom, and for peace exists. This hopeful outlook is itself possible in a violent, threatened world because the
Christian views the world from the center point of history,
the Cross, where God dealt redemptively with the crux of
the human problem.

While the Christian does not doubt God's ability nor His
final victory, he struggles to know and to implement God's
plan. Thankfully, there is an ongoing discussion of contem-
porary problems as Christians wrestle with agendas for action. As the publisher of the Crucial Questions series, we
earnestly hope that these volumes will contribute positively
to that discussion. Although the viewpoints expressed by
the authors in this series may not always be those of the
publisher, we are grateful for the opportunity to present
them to the public, and we trust that these volumes will
serve to stimulate Christians to fulfill their role as salt and
light in today's world.

A Time for
Compassion

A call to cherish and protect life.

Dr. RON LEE DAVIS with
JAMES D. DENNEY

Chapter One

A New Commitment to Life

Two Fates

For you created my inmost being;
   you knit me together in my mother's womb.
I praise you because
   I am fearfully and wonderfully made. . . .
                                    Psalm 139:13,14

The baby girl was born three months prematurely in a hospital in Minneapolis. She weighed only three pounds. The doctors told her parents that she was not expected to live, but promised to do everything possible to save her life. As scores of people around the country prayed for this tenuous new life, the most sophisticated medical technology available was employed to aid her fight for survival.

During the first six weeks of her life, which she spent enclosed in an incubator, she began to develop serious complications. Her weight began to drop. Her lungs had not had time to fully develop within the safety of her mother's womb, so she continually struggled with hyaline membrane disease and other pulmonary infections. Each day was a life-and-death battle.

She was kept on oxygen and monitored by machines and nurses twenty-four hours a day. Later, she was placed on a respirator and administered a powerful drug that temporarily paralyzed her entire body. At this point, one of the doctors took the father aside and told him, "You should begin to prepare your wife for the worst. We think your baby probably won't live much longer."

But the baby did live, and within a few more weeks the battle appeared to be won. She began to gain weight and strength, and was finally released to go home with her parents.

On the doctors' orders, the child was kept isolated from all visitors for a full year. During that time, she was not allowed out in public, even to visit with family or friends. Her mother, father, and grandmother alternated in shifts to give her the round-the-clock care she required.

After the first hard year was over, the child was able to go out and mingle with other children and adults. Today, she is a completely normal, happy, healthy young girl, full of life. The pediatric radiologist who cared for her through her struggle for life has shown the X rays of her lungs at medical conferences around the country, demonstrating to other physicians that it is indeed possible for a baby so premature and critically ill to survive.

The baby's name is Rachael LeeAnn Davis—our daughter.

Less than two years earlier, in a Boston hospital in late 1973, another baby, a boy, snuggled in the womb of his mother. Much like our Rachael, this baby had been growing within his mother for about six months. But this little boy would never be born. He was scheduled to be aborted.

The doctor prepared to inject a saline solution into the amniotic fluid that surrounded the baby. Normally this is a simple procedure. The concentrated salt solution causes the baby to convulse and die within the womb, after which the mother goes into labor and expels the dead baby.

First, however, the doctor must insert the hypodermic syringe and withdraw a little fluid to make sure the needle is correctly placed within the amniotic sac. If the fluid is clear, the abortion proceeds. A bloody tap, however, means the needle must be withdrawn and repositioned, lest the deadly saline solution be injected into the mother's bloodstream, sending her into fatal convulsions.

After repeatedly attempting to make the injection, each attempt producing a bloody tap, the doctor decided to use an alternate means of aborting the baby. He proceeded to perform a hysterotomy—that is, he surgically opened the mother's womb through an incision in her abdomen. This procedure is commonly used both for abortions and for live births in the event of complications. If the objective is a live birth, this procedure is called a cesarean section; if the objective is abortion, it is called a hysterotomy.

The doctor completed the incision, the pent-up fluids of the womb gushed out, and the doctor inserted his hand and began checking the unborn baby in the womb. Finding the baby alive, he proceeded to detach the placenta (the organ that supplies oxygen and nutrients to the baby), then waited several minutes for the baby to die of asphyxiation (lack of oxygen) within the mother. The baby's struggles ceased. Whether he was dead or simply unconscious from the combined effects of the mother's anesthetic and the lack of oxygen, no one knows.

The doctor then removed the seemingly lifeless baby and placed his hand on the baby's chest for a mere three to five seconds to check for life signs. Since the doctor clearly did not want to find any life signs (the object of this procedure, after all, is a dead baby), he failed to make even a minimal effort—such as taking just one minute to listen for heartbeat and breathing with a stethoscope—to determine whether or not the baby was truly alive or dead. He then placed the baby in a steel basin held by a nurse and instructed her to dispose of it.

No one who attended the abortion ever *really* knew if the baby was alive or dead; no one wanted to know.

The doctor who performed this abortion was later tried for manslaughter—not because he had performed an abortion (abortion-on-demand had been legalized nationwide just a few months earlier), but because when he had opened the womb and found a live baby, he tried to kill the baby by asphyxiation and, once he had removed the baby from the woman's body, he failed to adequately check the baby for signs of life.

A Massachusetts jury found this doctor guilty of manslaughter. That conviction was overturned by the state supreme court, and the doctor returned to the hospital and continued to practice medicine. The body of the baby remained in a bottle of formaldehyde in the Suffolk County morgue. No one was willing to sign a death certificate, so the baby could not be legally buried.

How is such a thing possible? How can the same medical skill and technology be put to such drastically different uses—the heroic effort to save our Rachael's life and the casual killing of an innocent baby boy? Why should these two babies, so similar in weight and gestational age, be treated to such different fates? Why death for one, life for the other? These two stories illustrate the moral and ethical schizophrenia that has taken hold of our nation since the legalization of abortion.

"Pro-Life": What Does It Really Mean?

> The only thing necessary for the triumph
> of evil is for good men to do nothing.
> Edmund Burke

I am pro-life. That is, I am *for life* with all of my heart and strength.

Normally when we hear people say they are pro-life, we

assume, "Oh, they're against abortion-on-demand." Yet I believe there is a much more inclusive and consistent meaning attached to the term *pro-life* than is generally assumed in our society.

Whenever we enable a woman with an unwanted pregnancy to choose nurturing or adoption, not abortion, we are being pro-life.

Whenever we choose to feed a hungry child, and thus fulfill the words of Christ, "Whatever you did for the least of these brothers of mine, you did for me," we are being compassionately pro-life.

Whenever we choose to care for even a few of the thousands of handicapped and retarded children and adults around us, we are being pro-life.

Whenever we seek to bring rehabilitation and the good news of Jesus Christ to someone in prison, or when we work to reform the prison system rather than allowing it to remain a seedbed for homosexuality and violence, we are being pro-life.

Whenever we help an alcoholic see his powerlessness without Jesus Christ, we are clearly being pro-life.

Whenever we seek to uphold the rights and dignity of women against the exploitation and predation of unequal pay and unequal opportunity, sexual harrassment, pornography, and abortion, we are being pro-life.

Whenever we become willing to study what the Scriptures teach us about trusting God for our security, rather than instruments of nuclear cataclysm, we are being pro-life.

Whenever we share with friends, neighbors, loved ones, or co-workers about the good news of resurrection life that God gives us through Jesus Christ, then we are being profoundly pro eternal life.

The tragedy of the pro-life movement as it has come to be known in our time is that, like the abortion policy it seeks to overturn, it goes only skin-deep. For many of us who claim to be pro-life, our commitment has become something we plaster on our bumpers, wear on our sleeves, recite with our mouths—but it has never reached our hearts. We have pro-life opinions. We may even have pro-life anger. But we do not have pro-life *compassion*, which comes only from a heart that is broken over the need and suffering of people.

Do we authentically listen to the humanitarian concerns of our opponents in the pro-choice movement—concerns about women with crisis pregnancies, about neglected and abused children, about the rising teenage pregnancy rate? Or do we simply write off people of pro-choice conviction with labels such as *murderer* and *baby killer?* By what right do we demand others change their hearts when our own hearts are filled with hatred?

Do we see women who suffer the trauma of unwanted pregnancy and abortion as perpetrators of a crime, or do we see them as victims? Have we offered our homes to unwed mothers seeking to raise their babies amid hardship and poverty, or have we simply marched in protest, carrying signs that read, "Wanted for Murder: 1.5 Million Women Who Had Abortions Last Year!"?

Over the years I have counseled scores of women who have struggled with the devastating guilt and grief that so often follow the act of abortion. Like the unborn children who died within them, these women are precious human beings, victims of a predatory society that prefers efficient killing to compassionate caring. These women come to our churches in desperate need of acceptance, healing, and for-giveness. How do we respond to that need? Are we truly for life, or are we merely *against* abortion?

Another tragedy of the pro-life movement is that our standards have not been applied with consistency. We say that the life of the unborn is infinitely precious, and it is; but what are we doing to save the lives of those babies who have already been born, but who are neglected and starving in parts of Africa, Asia, Latin America, and in our own inner cities in America? *Do we care as much for those lives we can see as those we can't?*

A consistent pro-life conviction calls us to the same way of living that Jay Kesler, then president of Youth for Christ, described when he said, "I am desperately concerned for unborn embryos who are being aborted, and the value of their lives. I am also desperately concerned about eight-year-old embryos who are starving to death, and the value of their lives." Human life is precious beyond measure, and the inestimable value of life must be understood in its full scope, not just in reference to the issue of abortion.

Pulling Down the Shades

> The child was diseased at birth,
> stricken with a hereditary ill:
> *poverty*, the most deadly and
> prevalent of all diseases.
> > Eugene O'Neill
> > *Fog*

Twice in the past three years, I have accompanied World Vision teams into remote, drought-scorched, cholera-plagued regions of Africa. There I have come face-to-face with little children who were made in the image of God, tender young lives with eternal souls. Their stomachs were swollen, either from malnutrition or worms. Their arms and legs were spindly. They were black children, but their hair was coppery orange, one of the signs of advanced malnutrition. I held these children in my arms, and I told them about Jesus, the One who has such a special love for children.

Some of the children I held in my arms died during my

stay in their villages. Many more have died since then. On several occasions, a World Vision doctor pointed out one child or another and said, "That boy will die of malnutrition in a day or two," or, "That little girl only has another week. She's beyond the best help we can give her." Of course, these doctors never gave up on *any* child—but their prognoses were invariably accurate.

I visited one African village where the infant mortality rate was 100 percent: All the babies born during the past year had died. Many died senselessly from measles or smallpox, diseases that are easily cured in America.

Tony Campolo tells the story of his first visit to Haiti, a chronically poor, hunger-plagued country very similar to the ones I visited in Africa. Haiti is a Caribbean nation, just 600 miles from America, where roughly half of all children die before the age of twelve.

One evening, Campolo went to a restaurant in Port-au-Prince. The waiter seated him by the window in front of the restaurant, took his order, and returned with his dinner. As he was being served, Campolo looked out the window and saw four starving street children with their noses pressed up against the glass. These children were not looking at Campolo but at the food-laden plate in front of him. These children were starving.

The waiter came over and pulled down the shade so Campolo couldn't see them. Then he said, "Don't let them bother you. Enjoy your meal." Campolo concludes, "As if it would have been possible to have enjoyed my meal after having seen those desperate children! However, don't we all do what that waiter did? Don't we all pull down the shade? Don't we all close out the hungry people of the world?"[1]

Yes, if we're honest, probably all of us would have to admit we've pulled the shade down on those around us who are dying and unwanted. We've shut our minds and hearts to the 40,000 children who starved to death *today*, who died so needlessly in the forgotten places of this world. Jesus said, ". . . Whatever you did for one of the least of these brothers of mine [the unborn, the neglected, the lost] you did for me" (Matthew 25:40). And I have to share my heart with you: I wrestle with that statement of Jesus. I wonder, will He one day say to me, "Ron, I was hungry and you never fed Me; I was naked and you never clothed Me; I was sick and you never visited Me; I was a stranger and you never gave Me a place to stay."

And what will I say then? "Lord, when did I see You hungry and not feed You? Or naked and not clothe You? Or sick and not visit You? Or a stranger and not give You shelter?"

"Ron, when you were so indifferent to all those little children you held in Africa."

For in the end, God will not evaluate our lives primarily by our ability to articulate fine points of doctrine or how forcefully we fought on various issues. No, we will be evaluated according to how we have responded to Jesus. And the Jesus we respond to is not an abstraction in the sky, but a Jesus who in a very real sense waits to be loved in the lives of the forgotten children—the last, the least, and the lost.

For many years, I've known there were 4,000 abortions taking place every day in America. But when I watched our little girl being born, I saw she was not "fetal tissue" but a sacred human life—and it really changed my heart.

I knew there were 40,000 children dying needlessly every day from hunger and disease. But when I held just a few of them in my arms, it really changed my heart.

I knew there were 3.5 billion people who have never heard the name of Jesus. But then I shared the name of Jesus with some children in Africa who had never heard His name before, and I saw how amazed they were that God would love them so much that He would send His only Son to die for them. And it really changed my heart.

We all need a change, a radical transformation; a skin-deep change is not enough. A change in opinion is not enough. We need a change of heart and a new commitment to life.

The time for compassion is *now*.

Source Notes

1. Anthony Campolo, *It's Friday, but Sunday's Comin'* (Waco, Tex.: Word Books, 1984), pp. 102, 103.

Chapter Two

The Aborting of Innocence

Laura's Story

I have sinned . . . for I have
betrayed innocent blood. . . .
Matthew 27:4

Death, once invited in, leaves
his muddy bootprints everywhere.
John Updike
Couples

My friend Laura is a thoughtful, articulate, well-educated young woman in her mid-thirties. This is her story, told in her own words:

I had my abortion in 1975, just before my twenty-sixth birthday. Basically, at the time, I was pro-abortion, because I had decided it was every woman's right to choose. I prided myself on being liberal minded, and I had accepted that a fetus was not a human life.

When I discovered I was pregnant, it was just a matter of going to the doctor to confirm it. He examined me and told me I was probably pregnant, but the test wasn't conclusive. He took for granted that I was going to have an abortion,

21

because I wasn't married. I wasn't even seeing the baby's father anymore.

I called the baby's father to talk about it. I felt he should be a part of the decision, but he didn't want anything to do with it. He hung up on me. So I had to make the decision myself.

I talked to some of my friends, and they said it was the only choice to make under the circumstances. I was also influenced in my decision by the kinds of trials I had gone through, growing up in a very troubled family. I had a bitter outlook on life because of the way my life had been, and I didn't want my child to have to live that way. Intellectually, I felt I had to have the abortion because I wasn't able to take care of a child.

I put off deciding for a while, so I was four months pregnant when I finally resolved to have the abortion. As quickly as I made the decision, I went to a clinic and set up an appointment. A few days later, when I went in for the procedure, I was surprised at how impersonal everything was. They just signed me in and told me where to wait. There was no counseling. No one even talked to me. It was just, "Sign this paper," and, "Do you want to be asleep or awake?" That was it.

Then they took me in for the procedure. It was really a very cold experience, very strange. There was no sensitivity. It was really detached.

They gave me a local anesthetic, and I was awake for the abortion. I remember it vividly. It was painful—more emotionally painful than physically painful. It was a suction abortion, and they had me on the table with my feet in the stirrups. They had just started the procedure when I asked them to stop the abortion. It had hit me suddenly, right in the midst of the procedure, that this was wrong. There was an actual physical sensation that I've often thought of as feeling my baby die inside of me. The doctor wouldn't stop the procedure. He said it was too late to stop.

There was one woman in the room who I guess felt sorry for me. She was trying to be nice, and she held my hand for the rest of the procedure. It was real agonizing.

In the recovery room, I got physically sick. There were several other women in the recovery room with me, either coming out of the anesthesia or waiting to go home. One woman had just aborted twins, and she began to talk to me. She chattered on about her abortion, about how having twins would have been too inconvenient for her. She was real happy, like she'd just been to a party or something. I had been feeling devastated inside ever since the middle of the procedure, when I wanted the doctor to stop. But sometime while I was talking to this woman, I just shut off all feeling. I closed off the experience and didn't begin to feel anything about it for several years.

I probably rationalized and used denial to avoid the fact that I had taken a life. A few years after my abortion, a friend of mine suffered a miscarriage. Whenever anybody talked about it, it was clear they acknowledged she had lost a child. In an abortion clinic, everybody's so careful not to refer to a *child* or a *baby*. The difference between people's attitudes toward a natural miscarriage and toward an abortion made it harder for me to hold onto my rationale.

About five years after my abortion, the guilt and anguish hit me catastrophically. It just broke me up. I don't know why it took so long for this emotional breakdown to come, but suddenly I felt I had murdered my child. This was a couple years before I came to know Christ. In fact, I think it was really this breakdown which started my search for God, for some kind of religious meaning in my life.

I was in real bad shape. I refused to go to anyone for help. I completely cut myself off from people. I took a year-and-a-half leave of absence from work because I just couldn't function. So many things were going wrong with my life. But during that time I began reading the Bible and talking to God, sometimes even screaming at God. I tried to work through my guilt feelings by myself for a while, but I didn't get very far.

At this time, I felt my whole life had fallen apart. I had gotten married, then divorced, in the space of about two years. I was an emotional wreck. The abortion and all the guilt I felt over it were the central problems of *all* my problems. That was the major issue out of many that led to my breakdown. I honestly wanted to die.

After a while, I started coming to church. Paradoxically, I had already made a decision to kill myself. I couldn't take any more of the mess my life had become. I couldn't live with issues like having had the abortion. But when I came into this church, I found something more meaningful than I had known before. The message and the things people were talking about in the service were really worthwhile. The congregation was very friendly, and they reached out. I kept coming to church, and began to know some people in the church very well. I began to see Christ *in* people, and I hadn't known that before. And that was the beginning of a long process of coming to know Christ in a real way.

I feel real strong in my relationship with Christ now. But it's been a real struggle. I've gone up and down a lot. There have been a lot of times when I couldn't understand how God could forgive me. Forgiveness has been real hard for me. I still don't know how to fully forgive myself for the abortion. I've made some progress toward forgiving myself, but I don't think I've ever had a single moment of feeling totally forgiven.

Emotionally, I equate abortion with murdering an innocent child. I see abortion as a very cowardly thing to do— not to bring my baby into the world, not to accept responsibility for that life. It's acting like God, making God's decision about life and death. And along with the guilt was a strange kind of grief. I felt I had lost a loved one I never got to know.

I've been through drugs, severe depression, divorce, and a lot of other really hard problems, but the abortion was the most devastating thing I've ever had to face. I'll get over the divorce and all the rest, but the memory of the abortion is something that will never go away.

It helps to realize that I had been deceived by pro-abortion claims. Sometimes I can tell myself that I wasn't fully responsible for that decision. It wasn't an informed choice. But there's something about a woman and her mother instincts. I knew I was killing my child. There's a basic animal instinct that mothers have, an instinct to protect their child. But I didn't protect my child, and that's something I'll always have to live with.

For a long time I couldn't figure out how I could have been so stupid. I'm not looking for excuses to justify my decision, but I know I bought into a lot of lies about abortion. And I guess I feel a little less stupid that I bought into the same deception a lot of women buy. But it makes me angry that the lie is still being sold, that people still allow abortion to continue.

Looking back, I realize I talked myself into believing something I really knew wasn't true. I told myself I couldn't take care of a baby. But I was working, I wasn't poor. I had a lot of personal problems. I had had some problems with drugs several years before. But I think I could have raised the baby, or at least given it up for adoption.

I didn't consider the alternatives. I didn't consider adoption, and I don't know why. I probably knew that if I brought a baby into the world, I wouldn't be able to give the baby up, and I was afraid of what might happen to the baby if I were to raise it. As distorted as it sounds, it seemed to me at the time that the selfish thing would be to have the baby.

Abortion is often real hard on the man involved, and I don't think that should be disregarded. I think the father is part of the process.

A few weeks after my abortion, the baby's father—who would have nothing to do with me at the time I was making the decision—came over to see me. He sort of wanted to pat my tummy and find out how the baby was doing. I mean, it was as if he had completely erased from his mind the fact that I was planning to have an abortion. When I told him I had gone ahead with the abortion, he became very angry, and he cried. It was real hard on him that his baby had been aborted. He had gone through this whole denial process and came over expecting me to still be pregnant.

A guy I knew was married once before. After their first baby, he and his wife discovered they were expecting a second child. They decided, just out of convenience, that they didn't want to have that child. They didn't want to bother with it financially, and they thought it would be a lot of trouble, raising two small children at the same time. So they aborted the child.

Afterwards, my friend and his wife had a lot of problems dealing with it. They both had nightmares about it, and she often woke up screaming. My friend had dreams in which the baby cried out for help, and he couldn't help the baby. Later, a third child was conceived and they considered abortion again, but they both realized they couldn't do it. Sometime after that baby was born, they got a divorce.

I've talked to a lot of women who have had abortions. Some experienced a lot of guilt afterwards, like I did. But some didn't seem to feel anything. I remember one who thought nothing of having an abortion. To her, it was like having a tooth pulled. Maybe she was asleep for her abortion and didn't feel what was happening to her. Maybe it would have been different for me if I had been asleep for my abortion, but I didn't like the idea of not knowing what was going on. I felt that if I was going to do this, I should be conscious of what was going on.

It's been more than ten years since my abortion, and I still haven't completely forgiven myself. But I've come a long way, and I think I owe that progress largely to the professional and pastoral counseling I've had. Also, talking through my feelings with other people helped, though I had a hard time finding someone who could really understand what abortion is like.

So many people have different attitudes about abortion. It's a political issue as well as a personal issue, and people will treat you differently according to their opinion of the *issue* of abortion. Some people will act as if you've committed the unpardonable sin, while others won't understand why you have all this turmoil over a "blob of tissue." It was so good to find some women who had been through an abortion, to have some heart-to-heart counseling with other women who understood.

One thing I did which has helped to relieve my sense of guilt is to teach a Sunday school class. The children I taught were about the age my child would have been. Some people may not understand that, but it was real helpful for me. I was able to give back to some other children what I had lost in my own life. I was able to give love to those children, and as they loved me back, it helped me feel I was not such a terrible person.

In a way that makes it hurt more, because I found out I'm really good with children, and now I realize I could have taken care of my own child. It wouldn't have been easy, I would have made mistakes, but I could have done it. That's a real hard thing to face. My fears before the abortion were unwarranted. They were foolish fears. One thing that makes the memory of the abortion so hard is knowing I gave up something that would have been the greatest joy of my life. Today I'm resigned to the fact that I will probably never have children of my own. But I have considered the possibility of adopting a child, perhaps a child with disabilities. It would be like getting a second chance to give love to a child.

I think it's real important for Christians to become politically active. I've often wondered why I haven't done that yet. I realize a part of the reason I haven't is that I'm ashamed of the abortion. I would have to come out and admit I had an abortion. But I think it's everybody's responsibility, and it's a Christian's responsibility, to help end legalized abortion.

I've never been real radical. I don't believe in bombing abortion clinics. But I think that whatever reasonable and legal things we can do to stop abortion should be done. I'm not opposed to demonstrations and marches and things like that. Whenever I see people carrying signs, I feel something's wrong with me because I'm not marching with them. I think if there had been demonstrators in front of the clinic where I had my abortion, I'd probably be a mother today. Something like that might have deterred me. Maybe I would have considered adoption.

Sometimes I look back on all the things I went through as a child, and I think, "Well, at least my baby was spared that." But there's never a moment that I think the abortion was okay, that it was justified because it spared my child some later suffering. If I had considered adoption, my child probably would have been spared that, anyway.

We have enough means to prevent pregnancies that there's no need to abort them. I'm still pro-choice. I just believe the choice has to be made at a different stage: before conception, not after a baby is already here.

Abortion's Other Victim

> If we deal unjust injury or violent
> death to others, we shall bring upon
> ourselves a death of the spirit—a
> violent death. Those who kill, die. And
> they die when they slay, not later.
>
> James T. Burtchaell
> *Rachel Weeping*

> The greatest harm is not to the body
> of the victim but to the soul of the
> perpetrator. Abortion harms the mother
> more than the fetus.
>
> Peter Kreeft
> *The Unaborted Socrates*

Across America, the aborting of the innocents takes place at a rate of 180 victims per hour—3 innocent victims every minute. But the tragedy of abortion extends beyond the death of innocents; it literally means the death of *innocence* for millions of women. It means guilt and psychological trauma that endure for years beyond the moment of abortion itself. In every abortion there is not one but two victims: the aborted child and the aborted mother.

For my friend Laura, abortion has been the central issue in her life for more than ten years. It is the single fact of her existence that prevents her from feeling whole and acceptable to herself and to God. It was the memory of her abortion that plunged her into years of depression and pushed her to the brink of suicide. Only the intervention of Jesus Christ in her life averted her self-destruction. Today, despite years of pastoral and psychological counseling and the support of many close Christian friends, she still has a great distance to go toward a complete sense of forgiveness.

Throughout my years as a pastor, I have counseled scores of women and couples who have struggled with the emotional aftermath of abortion. Again and again, I have seen the tragedy of Laura's experience repeated in other lives. A woman finds herself facing an unwanted pregnancy. Afraid and confused, she seeks counsel from friends, parents, or a doctor, and they answer, "Abortion." But once she enters the clinic, abortion ceases to be merely a word or an issue; it suddenly becomes a very real and personal *experience.*

In the process of abortion, a woman discovers the humiliation of being treated by clinical personnel as a collection of gynecological tissues to be "scraped out." It's the experience of lying on a table and having her cervix forcibly dilated and clamped open by metal instruments, so that a plastic tube can be thrust into her womb. It's the sudden rumble of the vacuum machine as it prepares to suck the life out of her belly. It's the palpable sensation of *violence* in the core of her being: the vibration, the tugging, the severing, the uprooting. It's the gritty feeling of the empty uterus closing around the suction tube as the procedure comes to an end. And it's the sudden rush of horror that comes with the realization, "I've just killed my baby!"

It has been said that a woman never forgets a pregnancy. In fact, many women who give birth after a previous abortion consider their firstborn to be their second child. The maternal instinct is so strong that it's not unusual for women, even after they have made the decision to abort, to carry on conversations with their baby, to carefully watch what they eat and drink, and even to exercise extra caution while they are driving to the abortion clinic. Abortion irreversibly impacts the lives of those who experience it, and that effect often manifests itself in the form of grief, guilt, depression, and other emotional problems.

In *The Ambivalence of Abortion*, Linda Bird Francke concludes from her research that abortion almost always damages or destroys the relationship between a woman and the father of her aborted child. She explains, "What had been pleasure became pain. What had been frivolous became heavy. Sex, which had brought intimacy and relief, brought memories of pain and guilt."[1]

Proponents of abortion have long tried to deny the psychological damage abortion so often causes. In his influential 1966 book *Abortion*, National Abortion Rights Action League founder Lawrence Lader writes, "It seems obvious that [psychological] damage from abortion is mainly the product of myth."[2] And pro-abortion psychiatrist Natalie Shainess states, "Never have I seen a case of genuine guilt or regret after abortion."[3] Such sweeping statements clearly say more about the ideology of the writers than about the facts.

Of course, it's true that not every woman experiences guilt in connection with an abortion. In abortion clinic waiting rooms across America, children—some as young as thirteen years old—wear half-lidded expressions, pop bubble gum, and seem blithely ignorant of what they are doing; many are doomed to be back two, three, or more times. Moreover, our society has so accommodated itself to abortion-on-demand and the resulting trivialization of human life that a "mature" thirty-five-year-old woman is able to say of her abortion, "I had no feelings about the baby. I had no emotional attachment to it. Hell, you can make one of those things every month."[4]

Research indicates that most women who seem genuinely unaffected by an abortion are either immature or emotionally disordered at the time of the procedure. As London psychologists C. M. B. Pare and Hermione Raven observed from their research, "The more mature and motherly the woman, the more likely [guilt] feelings were; and the more immature, psychopathic, or unmotherly, the more the patient was unaffected by a termination of pregnancy."[5] From my own experience as a counselor, I'm convinced that the experience of abortion rarely leaves a woman emotionally and psychologically whole.

The immense national problem of abortion induced guilt and psychological trauma was directly addressed in 1982 by the formation of WEBA, Women Exploited by Abortion.[6] Today, this organization has over 1,000 members nationwide, a great majority of whom have had firsthand experience with postabortion trauma. They offer their support to women going through emotional crises and publicize the psychological effects of abortion so that others will be warned before it's too late.

Another major organization that offers compassionate, understanding postabortion counseling is the Christian Action Council. Though the CAC's 240 Crisis Pregnancy Centers[7] nationwide are primarily devoted to offering alternatives to abortion, volunteers are trained to be caring and nonjudgmental, and women who decide to go ahead with their abortions after counseling are invited back for help with the emotional consequences.

Many abortion proponents blame religion for the guilt and trauma of abortion. One pro-abortion book states:

> Many people believe that "good" Christians and Jews are opposed to abortion. Therefore, these people reason, if a woman chooses to have an abortion she can expect to be punished by her pastor, her priest, her rabbi, and ultimately God.
>
> Why punished? Because those who are *opposed* to abortion have told anyone who will listen that women who have abortions are killing babies. Abortion, they say, is murder.... Clearly, if a woman's religion tells her abortion is murder she will experience conflict. The degree of conflict will vary according to how closely she identifies with the teachings of her religion.[8]

In the issue of abortion, as in so many other areas of life, faith is disparaged as an enemy of wholeness and good mental health.

Experience clearly shows, however, that guilt is not a religiously conditioned response to abortion. Laura's emotional struggle did not arise from religious beliefs; rather, the guilt she felt as a natural consequence of her abortion propelled her in a search for the religious meaning her life had been lacking. Atheists, agnostics, and people of nonchristian faiths experience pangs of conscience over abortion just as Christians do.

In Japan, for example, where over 50 million abortions have been carried out since legalization in 1952, maternal guilt and grief are assuaged by purchasing memorials for aborted "water babies" at certain Buddhist temples. These carved stone memorials often cost more than $600, while priests charge over $100 to regularly pray for the souls of the slain unborn. One of these temples has over 10,000 stone memorials standing in its courtyard. Clearly, the personal trauma that attends abortion is not a religious or cultural problem; it is a *human* problem.

Sometimes the aftereffects of abortion are more subtle, and potentially more dangerous, than an overt experience of guilt and remorse. The human mind is amazingly resourceful in defending itself from painful memories. Guilt feelings are sometimes driven deep into the recesses of the soul, to emerge years later in forms that are often difficult to recognize and treat. The guilt of abortion often surfaces as extreme depression, personality changes, mental illness, and even suicide. One woman describes an episode that was abruptly and inexplicably triggered several years after her abortion.

> All of a sudden, I was thinking about the abortion, and I couldn't understand why I was thinking about it. I started to become very anxious and just totally depressed. I cried a lot and had a lot of guilt feelings. And it shocked me . . . that I had actually interrupted a pregnancy. I think that what was so hard was my denial through the whole thing. I had a lot of physical symptoms related to this like dizziness. My pulse was very rapid, and I was short of breath. . . . I can remember crying a lot, and just a deep sense of hurting.[9]

Why does the trauma of abortion so often remain submerged for years, then explode without warning? How was the woman in the recovery room with my friend Laura able to chatter gaily about ending the lives of her unborn twins? How can women go to a clinic and say, "I want an abortion, even though I know it's murder," as one Planned Parenthood counselor reports she regularly hears?[10]

Denial and repression are powerful defenses that our minds call upon to exclude painful memories and awful truths from our consciousness. When we are faced with the inner conflict between the good person we see ourselves to be and some terrible thing we have done, our minds desperately seek some accommodation between these two incompatible images of ourselves. Psychologists view such fragmentation of the self-image as a sign of poor mental health. One young man tells how he and his girl friend sought to emotionally dissociate themselves from the guilt that followed her abortion:

> There was some kind of tug at the thought of the baby. It was not a fatherly one, but one of unease. We both cracked tasteless jokes about it months later, like how they disposed of it or whether it could have survived in salt water. Neither of us wanted to confront that we had wiped out something alive. So we played games. It's just like war when you end up calling the enemy gooks.[11]

Some abortion proponents actually encourage such mental, emotional, and moral incoherence. In a chapter called "What to Do About 'Bad' Feelings," one pro-abortion book offers this tranquilizing counsel:

> You may feel angry at yourself or your male partner or men in general. It can make you very nervous about lovemaking and even turn you away from sex for a while. Or you may feel very sad. Some part of you may be saying, "I'm bad," or "What I did was wrong," or even "I killed my baby" . . . .
>
> Allow yourself to mourn for the dead baby. Assuming, that is, that you feel you've killed a baby. Not everyone, by any means, feels that way. A lot of people who've given the subject a great deal of thought believe life begins at birth, not at conception. Legally speaking, they are right: a fetus is not a baby. However, from a religious point of view, there are many different opinions. . . .
>
> Many women find a way to make peace with the fetus. They feel the connection with the life inside them, and they begin a dialogue with it. An understanding is established so that when the abortion comes around, there's no blaming and no hard feelings. The memories afterward may be sad, but they also may be warm.
>
> Life comes and goes for all of us. Don't be too hard on yourself.[12]

Such advice leads to moral and emotional derangement: Mourn—but don't be too hard on yourself. Make peace with your baby, talk to it, then lovingly abort it—no blaming, no hard feelings. Looking back someday, you may even have warm memories about your aborted pregnancy.

Any human being who can entertain such a dissonant clash of feelings and thoughts at the same time is headed for serious trouble. As Curt Young observes,

> It is clear that abortion is a major hazard to the mental health of our citizenry. Rather than accept the responsibility they instinctively feel to love a newly conceived infant, parents suppress that instinct and misplace their guilt on the child, calling him or her "unwanted." Within themselves this argument is unpersuasive, however, and they come to experience abortion as violence against their own flesh and blood. Because it is.[13]

But there's hope for abortion's other victims. It's the hope of forgiveness, recovery, and wholeness in Jesus Christ. Christian compassion calls us to a ministry of loving and accepting those who suffer in the wake of abortion. While only God can forgive sin, He also uses *people* to express forgiveness and acceptance to those in emotional crisis. A woman who reaches for inner peace and wholeness after an abortion needs to feel the acceptance of others, and of the One who ". . . has authority on earth to forgive sins . . ." Jesus Christ (Luke 5:24).

The Christian approach to the trauma of abortion is very different from that usually offered by secular psychology or psychiatry. Secular approaches tend to encourage rationalization of guilt. The biblical way of forgiveness begins with a realization of responsibility and moves toward a genuine resolution of guilt. Thus, the first step toward wholeness is to squarely face the anguish of abortion. The woman should be encouraged by her counselor and closest friends to tell her story, to honestly express her pain. At the same time, she must be made to feel completely accepted by those with whom she shares herself.

Next, she must be helped to understand and accept an appropriate amount of responsibility for the abortion. Some women accept a disproportionately large share of guilt and see themselves as murderers; others seek to avoid responsibility, choosing to push all blame for the abortion choice onto others.

The appropriate amount of responsibility a woman should reasonably accept for her abortion is usually this: Under the pressure of difficult circumstances and conflicting advice, she chose to take her baby's life. The law and the culture around her strongly influenced her to believe that abortion is okay. Friends, family, and the father of her baby may have even put pressure on her to choose abortion. If she received any counseling prior to her abortion, it was probably the sort one would expect from those who make their living in the abortion industry: "The fetus looks just like a little ball of gauze. It's not human and it doesn't feel anything." Thus, out of a combination of panic, confusion, and misinformation, she has made a choice to take a human life—*but she has not committed murder.*

Opponents of abortion are often quick to sling the word *murder* at women who make this tragic choice. The dictionary, however, defines murder as "the crime of killing a person, especially with malice aforethought." Thus the word *murder* is not so much a description of an act as it is a condemnation of a person's intentions and moral responsibility. Abortion is almost always an act of desperation and confusion, not malice.

Once a woman has begun to accept appropriate responsibility for taking her baby's life, she must be allowed to feel sorrow. She knows death has taken place within her womb, the very sanctuary of life, and she knows a child has died within her because she demanded its death. As a mother, she condemns herself for willfully allowing her child to die. She sees herself as both mother and killer, and these images of herself are contradictory. The conflict this produces within the human soul is intense and enormously destructive.

So it's important that the woman find a new role for herself in the wake of abortion. She must begin to replace the image of herself as the killer of her child with a new image—the image of a bereaved mother. This can only happen as she is able to separate herself from the sin and death of the past, as she discovers release from the heavy responsibility of her abortion choice. The aborting mother is not alone in this, for we have all sinned, we are all guilty—and we all stand in need of forgiveness and release from the weight of our sins. Truly, the ground is level at the foot of the cross.

When a woman is able to see herself as cleansed and released from the responsibility for the death of her child, she becomes free to live again, free to accept herself as a person of worth and value, and free to give love to others. A new chapter opens in her life. She is fully aware that the past has truly happened, and that it contains some terrible realities. But she also knows that the past is over and God has a whole new future for her. This is a realistic response, a healthy response, free of denial, contradiction, and guilt.

Wholeness cannot come by excusing, minimizing, or avoiding truth and guilt. Rather, wholeness is the result of courageously working through the terrible truths of the past to an exciting new truth for the present and the future: God's love is unconditional, boundless, and completely encompassing. *Abortion is not the unpardonable sin.*[14]

Today, roughly ten to fifteen percent of all American women of childbearing age have had an abortion. Based on my experience in the counseling room, I would suspect these statistics hold true throughout the Church in America.

Thus, we may well find ourselves in situations in the Church where we will be tempted to soft-pedal the terrible truth of abortion for fear of stirring up painful memories. Yet I believe it is only the truth that will set us free.

I'm convinced that thousands of women will discover authentic freedom from guilt as we begin to communicate the truth that abortion is the taking of a human life, *coupled* with the truth that there is forgiveness and new life in the death and resurrection of Jesus Christ. John Powell confirms the reliability of this principle in his book *Abortion: The Silent Holocaust:*

> It is possible to speak about the monstrous and dehumanizing effects of legalizing this killing, and even to present the religious dimensions of this killing, without in any way passing judgment on the personal guilt of any of those in the audience.
>
> I remember one night a young woman, in a church-related group, coming up to me at the end of my presentation. She hugged me gratefully and whispered in my ear, "Thanks for what you said. Four years ago I had an abortion. I tried to look away, to forget what I had done. But it kept haunting me, like the skeleton in the closet. Tonight while you were talking I gave up my pretense of looking away. I faced it. I asked God to forgive me and to take care of the baby. Then I forgave myself. Tonight, for the first time since the abortion, I feel peace, deep peace, about the whole thing.[15]

For my friend Laura, the day of having complete peace about her long-past choice of abortion has not yet arrived. But I believe it will. She told me, "In dealing with my own guilt, I rely on God's forgiveness, though I don't know how He can forgive me. I intellectually tell myself what I am unable to accept emotionally, that God forgives me, no matter what I've done."

Laura is also beginning to discover some things she can do that are rebuilding her self-esteem and bringing her closer to wholeness. Because she now has no child of her own to love, she finds ways to show love to other children. She talks about adopting and about becoming active in the pro-life cause. She has taken an important first step by sharing her story with the readers of this book.

God is in the business of erasing sins and rebuilding lives. The life of David the psalmist is an inspiring example of God's loving power to reclaim people from their most disastrous mistakes. Second Samuel 11 and 12 tell how David, the king of Israel, falls first into sexual sin—the sin of adultery. Then, when the woman becomes pregnant with his son, David tries to cover up his first sin with the crime of murder: He arranges the death of his paramour's husband. King David is later stricken with paralyzing guilt and remorse for his sin, and it is during this experience of intense emotional anguish that David writes these lines from Psalm 51:

> Have mercy on me, O God,
> according to your unfailing love;
> according to your great compassion
> blot out my transgressions.
> Wash away all my iniquity
> and cleanse me from my sin.
>
> For I know my transgressions,
> and my sin is always before me.
> Against you, you only, have I sinned
> and done what is evil in your sight. . . .
> Hide your face from my sins
> and blot out all my iniquity.
>
> Create in me a pure heart, O God,
> and renew a steadfast spirit within me.
> Do not cast me from your presence
> or take your Holy Spirit from me.
> Restore to me the joy of your salvation
> and grant me a willing spirit, to sustain me.

Then I will teach transgressors your ways,
> and sinners will turn back to you.
Save me from bloodguilt, O God,
> the God who saves me,
> and my tongue will sing of your righteousness.

> Psalm 51:1–4; 9–14

And God blotted out David's sins and restored him to emotional wholeness and active service. God's epitaph on the life of David was not "Adulterer and Murderer," but, "... My servant David, who kept my commands and followed me with all his heart, doing only what was right in my eyes" (1 Kings 14:8). He removed David's bloodguilt, just as He wants to remove the guilt of every woman who struggles with a past abortion.

God doesn't want to destroy people for their sins, but to restore them from their sins. I see this process of restoration taking place in Laura's life. She is living proof of the words of my friend Dean Merrill, author of *Another Chance: How God Overrides Our Big Mistakes*. He writes:

> To be forgiven, to have our blot erased and forgotten, is a great gift.
>
> But to watch God fill the empty space, writing a new thing upon the tablet of our lives, is even greater.
>
> It is the final evidence that He does not hold a grudge, that He has not schemed some kind of residual punishment for us. His love is so complete that it does not stop until He has assured us that we are more than just tolerable in His sight; we are valuable.[16]

Laura is still sorting through her motives for wanting to help children and other people. To some degree, her desire to serve God and love others is part of a compulsion to atone for her sins. Yet I can also clearly see the grace of God seeping into her mind and heart. She is slowly discovering she doesn't need to work out her own atonement, because the atonement of Christ has completely covered all her sins. Laura is gradually learning to exchange guilt for gratitude. She is beginning to see her service to God not as a way of earning His forgiveness, but as a way of expressing her thankfulness that she is already cleansed and forgiven.

A Decision to Love

[God's] law requiring sexual faithfulness
in marriage to many people appears
oddly and needlessly restrictive. Why
not allow interchangeability, with men
and women enjoying each other freely?
We have the biological equipment for
such practices. But sex transcends
biology; it intertwines with romantic
love, need for stable families,
and many other factors. If we break
one law, gaining the freedom of
sexual experimentation, we lose the
long-term benefits of intimacy that
marriage is intended to provide.
Dr. Paul Brand
Fearfully & Wonderfully Made

Under current law, a woman may have an abortion for any reason—or no reason at all. Dr. Bernard Nathanson tells of one patient who came to him for an abortion because her due date conflicted with a planned vacation trip to Europe.[17] Abortions have occasionally been performed because prenatal testing disclosed the baby to be of the "wrong" sex. Abortion routinely takes place when a baby would interfere with a woman's career or when the parents feel vaguely unprepared to start a family.

Comparatively few women, however, view the abortion decision so casually. For most women who seek abortion, an unwanted pregnancy is not an inconvenience; it's a catastrophe. Many find themselves abandoned by the men responsible for their pregnancies. Others are thrown out of their homes by enraged parents. Some face poverty and the real fear of not being able to care for a baby. Many face the stigma of unwed motherhood. Panic, helplessness, shame, dread, and worry frequently form the emotional mix of an abortion decision. If we fail to acknowledge the pressures an unwanted pregnancy places on a woman's life, we trivialize the tragedy of abortion.

Looking back on the pressures that influenced her own decision, Laura offers a very personal perspective:

> I based my decision on the belief that I couldn't cope with unwed motherhood, and that I was sparing my child from future suffering. A lot of other women are making similar decisions today. I think this is something that should not be taken lightly. Women choose abortion because they feel they are faced with life-and-death situations. They are scared to death because they're not married or because they're poor or for some other reason.
>
> But whether or not the Supreme Court says abortion is okay, each woman has to decide for herself whether abortion is morally wrong or right. Having had an abortion, I'm now certain it's not morally right. I don't care if the child is going to be retarded or poor or fatherless or anything else. There are answers to those problems in life. But we don't solve problems by killing the children.

How, then, do we solve these problems?

We begin by making a decision to love and by teaching others to love. An accurate understanding of what the Bible means by the word *love* can transform people's understanding of the issues that surround the act of abortion. Biblically, the word *love* (in the original Greek, *agape*) refers not to an emotion but to an act of the will. Love, according to 1

Corinthians 13, is patient, kind, gentle, and self-sacrificing. Love protects and perseveres. This is not an unattainable, idealistic description of a set of warm feelings, but rather a practical way of responding to others regardless of our feelings. Love is a decision, not an emotion.

The act of abortion is obviously a raw denial of unconditional love, because it is a choice to kill rather than to care. But what many people fail to understand is that the act of sex, which often leads to unwanted pregnancy and abortion, can also involve a denial of genuine love. People regularly confuse love with sexual desire, which is one of the most deceptive of all human impulses. Only when people come to understand the difference between love and sexual desire will the reason for abortion—unwanted pregnancy—begin to be eliminated.

Though sexual attraction often masquerades as love in our society, it is actually an emotional tension, a kind of appetite. In marriage, sexual desire easily harmonizes with genuine love to produce a beautiful union between two people that is physical, emotional, and spiritual in its scope. The deceptive aspect of sexual attraction is that it combines not only with love, but with almost *any* powerful emotion. Combined with anger and hatred, sexual desire often produces the crime of rape. Combined with the despair of loneliness, sexual desire can result in meaningless sex with a virtual stranger, followed by even deeper loneliness and regret. Combined with the human vanity and the lust for conquest, sexual desire produces the sin of seduction.

All too often, two people come together in the belief that they love each other, when in reality they passionately, physically, selfishly *want* each other. Theirs is a desperate (though unconscious) search for a way to transcend loneliness, boredom, or low self-esteem. Erotic involvement dangles a false promise of emotional fulfillment.

When authentic love and commitment are lacking, the brief experience of fusion between two human beings is usually followed by the disappointing realization that they still remain strangers. They have exchanged a deep physical intimacy without the protective, genuine kind of love that would give the physical act of sex true meaning. Often the result of such intimacy is shame and estrangement. And there are other consequences as well, such as sexually transmitted disease and unwanted pregnancy.

Those of us who are Christian parents naturally want to prevent our children from having to learn these truths the hard way. We are awakening to the corrosive influence our culture is having on the attitudes of our young people (and, yes, on ourselves as well), and we wonder what we can do. The place to begin is in our own homes.

We need to look within ourselves and ask: "Do I have a healthy attitude toward sex? Can I talk to my children about sex without embarrassment? Do my children see me as someone they can talk to anytime about any problem or question? Am I a friend to my children? Am I showing affection to my children? Am I affirming them and building their self-esteem so they will have the inner strength to stand when temptation comes?"

In the public schools, young people are exposed to sex-education programs that describe the essential mechanics of sex, reproduction, and contraception without any moral or ethical framework, supposedly to insure that no one person's value judgment intrudes on anyone else's. Yet the decision to make *no* statement about sexual ethics is itself a statement suggesting that morality is irrelevant in today's world.

Our churches can have a strategic role in educating our young people in a logical, biblical framework for sexual responsibility. We need to look at our churches and ask: "Does my church provide frank biblical teaching about human sexuality? Does my church teach the biblical truth that sexual expression within marriage is beautiful and elevating?"

Then, finally, we must look to the world and ask ourselves: "How can I become involved in communicating God's wholeness to a broken world and God's love to an unloving world?" In the Sermon on the Mount, Jesus calls us to become salt and light in our society. Salt is a preservative; thus we are called to be a kind of preservative in our world, penetrating and illuminating the world with the light of Christlike love—love that is rooted not in the emotions but in the will.

We become salt and light in the world as we become involved in the lives of our neighbors, co-workers, and friends. We have an opportunity to help preserve and illuminate others every time we have a conversation during a coffee break, over lunch, in the car pool, at the checkout counter, on an airplane, or after dinner with friends. In gentle, patient, nonargumentative ways, whenever the conversation turns to issues such as abortion, teenage sex, the pressures of parenthood, or "the mess the world is in today," we can inject our biblical world view into the discussion. We can explain the difference between the world's love and the unconditional love of God. We can counter the worldly cynicism that sees abortion as a necessity, and we can seek to build a world that heals parents instead of destroying children.

The pro-abortion argument hinges on the contention that abortion is inevitable and necessary in our society, and that we therefore must make abortion legal and safe so women can have control over their own bodies. But the truth is that abortion is far from inevitable, necessary, or safe. We have within our reach a range of workable, sensible alternatives to abortion by which both men and women can exercise authentic control over their bodies. For example, if two people decide they don't want to have a baby, they may practice abstinence, sterilization, or contraception.

Contraceptives currently in use by both men and women are known to be extremely effective, and in those instances when they do fail, there are still two options available: offering the child for adoption and taking loving responsibility for the child.

Ultimately, we must begin to acknowledge that sex is not merely a form of recreation; rather, sex is a positive act of commitment to another person, entailing certain predictable risks and responsibilities. People have an unrealistic expectation that they should have the choice to do whatever they want without any consequences—even the logical consequences of biological nature. The fact is that every action in life has consequences. Sexual intercourse has a natural, predictable tendency to bring about children. It does not seem unreasonable to expect our society to accept this simple fact.

Advocates of abortion choice are understandably troubled by the cause-and-effect relationship between abortion and guilt. Karen Mulhauser, executive director of the National Abortion Rights Action League, calls pro-life advocates "the compulsory pregnancy people," and accuses them of seeking to inflict "misery and shame on the poor and the pregnant." In a 1979 NARAL fund-raising letter, she writes, "Make no mistake about it, much of the controversy reflects not just religious scruple but a yearning for moral punishment." But before we dismiss these words as just so much inflammatory rhetoric, we should re-examine our own attitude toward women with unwanted pregnancies and the babies they carry within them.

We should never suggest that a baby is punishment for sexual sin. Psalm 127:3 tells us that children are a *reward* from the Lord. All life is a gift from God, the author of life, and even though people sin, fail, and make mistakes, God does not. A baby is a miracle of God's grace, no matter what the circumstances of its conception—even if the circumstances involve an act of disobedience to God. So-called unplanned pregnancies are only unplanned by people; God has a plan for even the most unwanted child.

A few years ago, my friend Sandy was nineteen years old, unmarried, and in love with a young man named Dave. As Dave and Sandy became more and more deeply involved, they began to discuss the future. "I've never loved anyone like I love you," he told her, "and I promise I'm going to spend the rest of my life making you happy. You can count on that."

A short time later, Sandy discovered she was pregnant. When she told Dave, he was stunned. "Well, what do you want me to do, Sandy?"

"Well. . . ," she hesitated, trying to read his thoughts. "I thought we could get married and. . . ."

"No, that's out of the question," Dave interrupted. "Marriage is just not in my plans right now. It seems to me there's only one thing for you to do. And don't worry about the money. I'll help you pay for it."

"You mean—an abortion?"

"It's the only way."

Sandy struggled for several days with her decision. She talked to some friends in the church, spent time in the Bible, and finally became convinced that the new life growing inside her was a human being, created in the image of God. She decided not to have the abortion. Then she told Dave her decision.

"Dave," she said, "I'm going to keep this baby, and I want to share the baby with you. You once told me you loved me, and that you were going to spend the rest of your life making me happy. I want to know if you really meant that."

"I need some time to think," he said. But it didn't take him long. The next day, he called her and told her he didn't want to see her anymore.

Feeling she had no one else to turn to, Sandy came to us, and we took her into our home. My wife, Shirley, went through the childbirth classes with her, drove her to the hospital, and coached her through labor and delivery. Sandy gave birth to a beautiful little girl and continued to live with us for several months more. I'm convinced that we and our children were blessed even more than Sandy by the experience of helping her through those hard months and seeing a beautiful new life come into the world.

In Sandy's story, there is a clear contrast between the way the world loves and the way God calls us to love. Dave talked about love, but it was Sandy who made a *decision* to love. Dave's love was conditional, rooted in his emotional attraction for Sandy, but Sandy's love was unconditional and did not fail. She literally loved her baby into the world. But had she chosen differently, her child would now be nothing more than an ache of regret and sorrow.

Abortion destroys an innocent child, but the tragedy doesn't end with the life of the unborn. Long after the procedure is over, the act of abortion goes on killing—destroying a mother's love, a mother's soul, a mother's innocence. The fight for life is a compassionate struggle to save *all* the victims of abortion, both the unborn and the women who give them life.

Source Notes

1. Linda Bird Francke, *The Ambivalence of Abortion* (New York: Random House, 1978), p. 47.

2. Lawrence Lader, *Abortion* (Boston: Beacon Press, 1966), p. 23.

3. Natalie Shainess, "Abortion Is No Man's Business," *Psychology Today* (May 1970), p. 20.

4. Francke, *Ambivalence*, p. 104.

5. From "Follow-Up of Patients Referred for Termination of Pregnancy," a 1970 article in the British medical journal *Lancet;* quoted in *Abortion: The Personal Dilemma* by R. F. R. Gardner (Grand Rapids: Eerdmans, 1972), p. 211.

6. For the address of a local WEBA chapter, contact Women Exploited by Abortion, P.O. Box 267, Schoolcraft MI 49087, (616) 679-4069.

7. For the address of a local Crisis Pregnancy Center, check the local Yellow Pages under "Family Planning Information Centers" or "Birth Control Information Centers" or contact Christian Action Council, 701 W. Broad Street, Suite 405, Falls Church, VA 22046, (703) 237-2100.

8. Carole Dornblaser and Uta Landy, Ph.D., *The Abortion Guide: A*

Handbook for Women and Men (New York: Playboy Paperbacks, 1982), pp. 23, 164, 165.

9. Curt Young, *The Least of These* (Chicago: Moody Press, 1983), p. 63.

10. Francke, *Ambivalence*, p. 32.

11. Ibid., p. 137.

12. Maria Corsaro and Carole Korzeniowsky, *A Woman's Guide to Safe Abortion* (New York: Holt, Rinehart and Winston, 1983), pp. 57, 61, 62.

13. Young, *Least of These*, p. 69.

14. For a more complete discussion of God's forgiveness, self-forgiveness, freedom from guilt, and the healing of painful memories, *see* chapters 1–5 of *A Forgiving God in an Unforgiving World*, by Ron Lee Davis with James D. Denney (Eugene, Ore.: Harvest House, 1984).

15. John Powell, *Abortion: The Silent Holocaust* (Allen, Texas: Argus Communications, 1981), p. 101.

16. Dean Merrill, *Another Chance: How God Overrides Our Big Mistakes* (Grand Rapids: Zondervan, 1981), p. 125.

17. Bernard N. Nathanson with Richard N. Ostling, *Aborting America* (Garden City, N.Y.: Doubleday, 1979), p. 230.

Chapter Three

The Meaning of Life

At War With Death

Any man's death diminishes me,
because I am involved in mankind.
John Donne
Devotions

The last enemy to be destroyed
is death.
1 Corinthians 15:26

Paul John Davis was my only brother. As a Christian coach, he had an enormous impact on the lives of many young men who were trained in the basketball clinics he held around the country. He was active in the Fellowship of Christian Athletes and also had an important teaching ministry among the mentally retarded. Paul was a devoted Christian husband and father, and his number-one goal in life was to become more like Christ as he built faith and healthy Christian self-esteem into his family.

Today, as I write these words, it has only been a few months since Paul's death from cancer at the age of forty-one. Though I have a sense of peace in knowing that God is sovereign over the death of my brother, Paul, it's a loss that cuts deeply and will never completely heal. I'm angry with death. It has robbed me of my best friend.

Over the years, death has snatched many close friends from my life. I still feel grief over the loss of my father, who died some twelve years ago. Death has also taken many of my classmates, co-workers, and Christian friends. I've officiated at funerals for young people and children too numerous to count. As I think back over all those lives that ended too soon, I have to say that I am at war with this destroyer called death; to just say I'm pro-life is too mild a term. I'm *angry* with death, and I believe we as Christians must be committed to struggling against this enemy with all the weapons at our disposal.

I believe when we say we are pro-life we must hold all human life to be incalculably precious and worthy of redemption at any cost. For that is the heart of the Christian gospel: Despite our sin, God valued all humanity so much that He sacrificed His only Son to purchase our eternal lives (*see* John 3:16). Clearly, God places a different price on human life than the culture around us. To the world, human life is a plentiful commodity on a fluctuating market; generally, it sells pretty cheaply. But to God, a human being is not merely valuable, but invaluable. Human life is quite literally priceless. That is what we mean when we talk about the sanctity of life. This doesn't mean we worship life, but that we reverently cherish life because of the infinite value God has invested in it.

What, then, is this fleeting, intangible, priceless thing called life? Perhaps we can only begin to sense the wonder and the miracle of human life when we have squarely faced the horror that is death.

The apostle John sketches a compelling portrait of death in the story of the raising of Lazarus. Imagine the scene of John 11 with me: There was grief and mourning in the little village of Bethany. Lazarus had been dead four days when Jesus and His weary followers trudged into town. He was met first by Martha and later by Mary, the two sisters of Lazarus. Both of these women told Jesus, "Lord: if you had been here, our brother would not have died ..." (John 11:21). Jesus' confident reply: "Your brother will rise again.... I am the resurrection and the life ..." (John 11:23,25).

Later, however, as He approached the tomb of Lazarus, He became deeply saddened, groaning within Himself with sorrow over the death of His friend Lazarus. Amazingly, John 11:35 records, "Jesus wept." Think of it: *Jesus wept!* And like those who saw Him weeping, we marvel, "See how Jesus loved him!" The man who moments before had called himself the resurrection and the life wept at the threshold of the grave! I've often wondered why. Certainly, Jesus knew He had the power to raise Lazarus, even though the man had been dead four days. He even stated His clear intention to do so: "Your brother will rise again." Why, then, did Jesus weep if He knew that Lazarus would live again?

Perhaps it's because Jesus knew—far better than any of us can know—the true nature of death. He knew that Lazarus had been swallowed by the greatest enemy of mankind. Jesus, who came into the world to do battle with death, understood His adversary well. To Jesus, death was not "an untimely frost" or "a sleep ... a consummation devoutly to be wished," as Shakespeare has described it. No, death is a destroyer. It is, as J. G. Neihardt once wrote, "the grisly Thing ... the gray Perhaps." In 1 Corinthians 15:26, Paul calls death an enemy, "the last enemy to be destroyed." Jesus came to destroy the grisly thing, to penetrate the gray perhaps—to free those, as Hebrews 2:15 says, "... who all their lives were held in slavery by their fear of death."

This was Christ's central ministry on earth: destroying death and bringing forgiveness, hope, and new life to lost and dying human beings. If that was His mission, then it must also be the mission of those who call themselves

Christians and bear His name. The battle against death must be our battle, too.

Pagan Justice vs. Christian Justice

Speak up for those who cannot speak
for themselves, for the rights of
all who are destitute. Speak up and
judge fairly; defend the rights of
the poor and needy.

Proverbs 31:8,9

Is this law just? That is, does
it coincide with the Law of God,
the Constitution of the Universe?

Rev. Theodore Parker

If the abdominal wall of the pregnant
woman were transparent, what kind
of abortion laws might we have?

Dr. Bernard Nathanson
Aborting America

The abortion industry in America was created with the stroke of a pen on January 22, 1973. That pen was wielded by Justice Harry Blackmun of the United States Supreme Court in the case of *Roe vs. Wade*. It was the most sweeping judicial decision in American history.

Roe vs. Wade stunned the nation by preempting a volatile and ongoing national debate. Though Supreme Court decisions historically tend to be cautious and narrowly focused, this decision was so devastatingly broad in scope that even the pro-abortion forces were left breathless. In one day, every last jot and syllable of abortion legislation in America was suddenly erased. Gone were statutes that had stood for two centuries, descended from English common law, as

well as the few remaining ordinances in such abortion cita-
dels as California, New York, and Washington, D.C.

When America awoke to the fact that all abortion regula-
tion had suddenly ceased to exist, there was an immediate
open season on the unborn. Suddenly America had the
most permissive abortion laws on the planet. By the end of
1973, over 200 bills were introduced in state legislatures in a
frantic effort to put some controls—any controls—on abortion. Some state legislatures took as long as two years to
enact laws that would pass the Supreme Court test. During
the gap between *Roe vs. Wade* and the enactment of new
laws, the unborn could be aborted at any stage and for any
reason, no matter how frivolous. The decision kicked off the
longest, angriest period of civil strife in America since the
Vietnam War.

The court's decision divided a normal 270-day pregnancy
into three 90-day trimesters and held that during the first
trimester, the state could not prohibit or regulate abortion
in any way.[1] During the second trimester, the state could (if
it so chose) regulate abortion in ways "related to maternal
health." During the third trimester, the state could (if it so
chose) regulate or prohibit abortion, "except where necessary, in appropriate medical judgment, for the preservation
of the life or health of the mother." In effect, *Roe vs. Wade*
made abortion legal virtually until the last moment before
birth. In most states, abortionists now practice their trade
with fewer legal restrictions than barbers.

Blackmun's written decision in *Roe vs. Wade* is, like most
Supreme Court decisions, a lengthy and detailed document
that discusses the historical and legal rationale on which it is
based. I won't dwell in detail on *Roe vs. Wade* in this book,
since the decision has been thoroughly explored by others.[2]
But there are a few major aspects of the court's decision that
go to the heart of the abortion debate and are still not fully
appreciated by most people.

In his written opinion, Justice Blackmun offers an amazingly selective reading of the history of abortion. The historical framework of *Roe vs. Wade* is derived from the pagan practices and attitudes of the pre-Christian era. The highest ethical statements of Greek and Roman philosophy are airily swept aside in the court's quest for the lowest common denominator of pagan social conscience. The court even disdains the 2,400-year-old Hippocratic oath, which explicitly states, "I will not give to a woman an abortive remedy."[3]

In the opening section of his opinion, Blackmun writes, "Greek and Roman law afforded little protection to the unborn. . . . Ancient religion did not bar abortion." Blackmun fails to note that Greek and Roman law also gave fathers absolute life-and-death power over their children. At birth, newborn infants were placed before the father to be inspected for defects. He had the choice to either accept and name the child or cast the child out to die from exposure and be ravaged by animals. Older children could legally be sold into slavery.

It wasn't until the Christian gospel began to penetrate Greek and Roman culture that these practices were abolished. Yet Blackmun is completely silent about Christian history and values, upon which our highest and most compassionate laws and ethics are based. It is as if the last two millennia of Christian history had never existed.

Historically, the Christian Church has never had any doubts about the personhood of the unborn. *The Didache*, a first- or second-century Christian document, states firmly, "You shall not slay a child by abortion." The first-century Epistle of Barnabas, attributed to Paul's missionary companion, states, "You shall not destroy your conceptions before they are brought forth, nor kill them after they are born." Second-century Church father Quintus Tertullian commented, "To forbid birth is only quicker murder. It makes no difference whether one take away the life once born or destroy it as it comes to birth. He is a man who is to be a man. The fruit is always present in the seed."

Christians have historically viewed all human beings as being made in the image of their Creator at conception. Thus John Calvin observed, "The unborn child, though enclosed in the womb of its mother, is already a human being, and it is a heinous crime indeed to rob it of the life it has not yet begun to enjoy." The Supreme Court did not consult the Christian heritage of Western civilization in its search for an historical perspective on abortion. Instead, it cited the brutish attitudes of a pagan age—and then presented us with a brutal, pagan law.

James T. Burtchaell notes that the Blackmun decision "reproduces intact the interpretation of Cyril Means, Jr., legal counsel to the National Association for the Repeal of Abortion Laws, . . . and Lawrence Lader, NARAL founder: together they are cited fourteen times by the Court. The history they offer has not been flattered by critical scrutiny."[4] In other words, the court's decision—which Blackmun claimed was arrived at "by constitutional measurement, free of emotion and of predilection"—was based on arguments lifted straight from the pamphlets of the most passionately pro-abortion group in the country.

From ancient history, Blackmun moved next to a discussion of the Constitution itself. There, between the lines, Blackmun claimed to find a special "right of privacy" that largely prevents the state from interfering in an abortion decision. At first glance, a constitutional right to privacy seems only fitting, for who doesn't feel constitutionally entitled to privacy? Yet Blackmun's use of this term is both technical and peculiar: He is not referring to privacy within the home, but to privacy between a woman and her doctor. All decisions regarding abortion are left to the doctor's "best clinical judgment," even though 98 percent of all abortions are for nonmedical reasons, and are thus outside the training and experience of most physicians.[5]

What is the source of this newly discovered privacy doctrine that gives doctors such complete sovereignty over the abortion decision? The language of the Constitution nowhere supports it. Rather, Blackmun says this "right" is an "emanation of the penumbra" of the Bill of Rights. A *penumbra*, according to the dictionary, is "the partial shadow surrounding a complete shadow, as in an eclipse." Thus, this peculiar right of privacy that Blackmun summons like a spectre from his reading of the Constitution is in fact a shadow right, cast by the court's decision to eclipse the rights of the unborn.

There were two dissenting justices to *Roe vs. Wade*, and they were particularly critical of Blackmun's shadow right. "To reach its result," wrote Justice William Rehnquist, "the Court necessarily has had to find . . . a right that was apparently unknown to the drafters of the Amendments." And Justice Byron White, who called the decision "an exercise of raw judicial power," observed, "the Court simply fashions and announces a new constitutional right for pregnant mothers . . . with scarcely any reason or authority for its actions."

But the court did more than invent new rights for aborting mothers and their doctors. It shrugged from its shoulders the massive weight of legal tradition that had favored the unborn for centuries. But before it could do so, the court had to confront the Fourteenth Amendment: "No state . . . shall deprive any person of life, liberty, or property, without due process of law." Clearly, the crucial question before the court was: Is the fetus a person or not? Blackmun acknowledged the dilemma this question posed: "If this suggestion of personhood [of the fetus] is established, [the pro-abortion] case, of course, collapses, for the fetus' right to live would then be guaranteed specifically by the [Fourteenth] Amendment."

Blackmun and his Supreme Court brethren devised a solution to the personhood problem: They invented a dichotomy between "human beings" and "persons." Thus the court semantically fashioned a class of human beings who were in effect "unpersons."

The framers of the Fourteenth Amendment would certainly have been mystified by the idea that a human being does not equal a person. In fact, the amendment was enacted shortly after the Civil War to ensure that *no* human being would ever again be denied life and freedom, as had happened to blacks under slavery. The word *person* in the amendment was meant to be an inclusive term; Blackmun redefined it as an exclusive term to keep unborn human beings outside the pale of constitutional protection.

Blackmun concluded with an equivocation worthy of the rhetorical "what is truth?" of Pontius Pilate: "We need not resolve the difficult question of when life begins. When those trained in the respective disciplines of medicine, philosophy and theology are unable to arrive at any consensus, the judiciary, at this point in the development of man's knowledge, is not in a position to speculate as to the answer." Like Pilate, Blackmun and his brethren of the court held the power of life and death over innocent blood. Like Pilate, they chose to dispense ambiguity instead of justice and to crucify the innocent.

When does life begin? Even if we grant Blackmun's claim that this question can't be answered, the court's decision was clearly reckless. Philosopher Peter Kreeft of Boston College likens the Blackmun decision to the rash act of a hunter who shoots at a sudden movement in the bushes, not knowing whether he would be killing a deer—or another hunter.[6] Such disregard for human life (whether in a deer hunter or a Supreme Court decision) is neither prudent nor moral. Life must always be handled with care. In Deuteronomy 30:19, God through Moses told the people of Israel, ". . . I have set before you life and death, blessings and curses. Now choose life, so that you and your children may live." The Supreme Court, however, chose death—and today the children are dying by the thousands.

But is the question of when life begins really such a difficult question, as Blackmun contends? I'm convinced it is not a difficult question now, nor was it in 1973. In fact, any high-school biology student could have advised the court on this scientific fact: The life of a human being begins at conception.

The Facts of Life

The history of a man for the nine
months preceding his birth is probably
far more interesting, and contains
events of greater moment, than
all the three score and ten years
that follow it.
Samuel Taylor Coleridge

A person's a person, no matter how small.
Dr. Seuss
Horton Hears a Who

Human life, as biochemist Isaac Asimov observes, is an unbroken continuum from conception to death. He writes, "You might have been born on a certain day of a certain year. You may even have a record of the exact hour, minute, and second in which you drew your first breath, but is that the moment you came into existence? It is only the moment you emerged from the womb. You existed as a genetically distinct individual from the moment of conception some nine months before."[7]

Other leading scientists concur. Dr. Jerome Lejeune, professor of genetics at the University of Descarte in Paris, is the renowned biologist who first identified the genetic basis of Down's Syndrome. Testifying before the Senate Judiciary Committee in 1981, he said, "When does a person begin? ... Each individual has a very neat beginning, the moment of its conception. The human nature of the human being from conception to old age is not a metaphysical contention. It is plain experimental evidence." Similarly, Dr. Hymie Gordon, chairman of the medical genetics department of the Mayo Clinic, testified, "By all the criteria of modern molecular biology, life is present from the moment of conception."

Just prior to conception, there are two distinct cells, produced by two separate human beings. Each cell, the sperm and the egg, contains twenty-three chromosomes; that is, each contains only half of the forty-six chromosomes needed to make a human being. But at the precise moment when the sperm joins with the egg, a single individual cell (called a *zygote*) suddenly exists, possessing all forty-six chromosomes. Within the first hour after conception, the nuclei of the two cells have fused and the entire design of a uniquely individual human being is completely established.

Though just a single microscopic cell, the human zygote is irrefutably a living human organism, and if allowed to proceed naturally, without the interruption of accident, disease, or harmful intervention (such as abortion), this life can reasonably be expected to fulfill its potential for some seventy, eighty, or more years. Nothing will ever be added to this cell that can make it more human than it already is. This is not a religious idea or a philosophical theory; this is a biological fact of life.

Despite the scientific evidence, abortion proponents recoil at the thought that a single fertilized cell should be accorded the status of a person with a right to life. In *The Unaborted Socrates*, Peter Kreeft resurrects the ancient Greek philosopher for a dialogue with an abortionist named Dr. Herrod:

> *Herrod:* . . . Whenever a person begins, it just can't be as early as fertilization. Just look at that zygote: a single cell with no brain, no nervous system, no consciousness, no heart, no face—don't you feel the utter absurdity of calling *that* a human being?

Socrates: Because it doesn't look at all like a human being?

Herrod: Of course.

Socrates: But our question is not what it looks like but what it *is*.[8]

Science can describe (but not yet explain) how a fertilized egg grows into a fully formed adult. It begins with the forty-six chromosomes in the cell. The chromosomes contain the genetic code, which is in the form of a long, coiled molecule called DNA. The code describes in astounding detail the entire physical makeup of the individual, from the intricate structures of the cells to the specialized functions of the organs to the color of hair and eyes and the features of the face.

DNA is actually a kind of submicroscopic sentence written in a chemical alphabet of only four letters called nucleotides. A single strand of human DNA is composed of about 5 billion pairs of nucleotides, and contains about as much information as 10,000 volumes the size of this book. Mysteriously and miraculously, this array of genetic information is translated into a three-dimensional structure: the human body.

A human body starts as a single fertilized cell, which divides into two cells. These two divide into four, then sixteen, and on and on. By the time the embryo numbers thirty-two cells (about four days after conception) it forms a raspberry-shaped cluster that is snuggled into the lining of the uterus. It is already arranged into an inner mass and an outer layer, suggesting the arrangement of the organs and outer tissues of the human body.

Over the coming weeks of growth, the DNA blueprint exerts command over an amazing complex of functions, causing the cells to arrange themselves in purposeful ways. Symmetrical ripples, dimples, and folds appear, forming the basis of embryonic organs. The cells begin to differentiate into the more than 200 cell types that make up nerve, bone, organ, and other tissues of the human body. Though the embryo weighs only one-thirtieth of an ounce at the end of the first month of life, it already exhibits a functioning brain and beating heart.

By the end of the second month, the unborn human being is an inch and a half long and has assumed a definite baby shape. The arms and legs, fingers and toes, facial features, and genitalia are clearly formed. The baby begins to make movements at six weeks, experiences both sleep and wakefulness, and will continue to be in almost constant motion throughout its wakeful periods in the womb.

At three months, the unborn baby is four inches long and weighs one ounce. His skeletal structure has taken form. Moving his arms and legs like a swimmer, he energetically propels himself about, performing acrobatic maneuvers in the amniotic sea. By ten weeks, he is clearly sensitive to cold, heat, sound, light, touch, taste, and pain. A loud noise or a jolt to the mother's abdomen will cause the baby's heartbeat and respiration[9] to race—a reaction identical to the anxiety reaction of an adult human being. Experiments show that a fetus at this stage can learn and can experience boredom, excitement, and fear.

At four months, his movements are felt by the mother. He weighs four ounces and is in all respects a tiny but completely formed human being. He has begun to suck his thumb. By this time, the unborn baby is clearly self-aware. "A sixteen-week-old fetus will kick and squirm if prodded by a needle," observes Dr. William A. Nolen. "That, it would seem to me, is very simple evidence that the fetus is self-conscious. Perhaps a sixteen-week-old fetus does not spend time . . . thinking about the meaning of life or musing on the works of Plato, but neither does a two-year-old toddler."[10]

At five months, he weighs a full pound. His eyes now open and close, and he sometimes gets the hiccups. The brain activity of a twenty-week-old fetus, as measured by electroencephalograph, is virtually identical to that of a newborn baby. He can still be aborted on demand for another seven weeks.

At six months, he weighs two to three pounds, measures fourteen inches long, and is considered viable by Supreme Court standards (that is, he can probably survive outside the womb). From now until birth, this delicately formed human being will grow, kick, wriggle, and dream as the finishing touches are added to his elaborate nerve and lung systems. Yet 6 percent of all abortions (about 96,000 per year) are performed at this stage, twenty-eight weeks or later, despite the fact that premature babies have survived birth as early as twenty-one or twenty-two weeks.

Nowhere along the entire prenatal spectrum can we find any magical moment we can identify as the threshold of "personhood." The starting point of every human being is conception itself. As Bernard Nathanson comments,

> The *science* of the abortion debate is simply not in dispute. Personhood does not really depend upon consciousness, but upon people recognizing the human life that is there among us, beyond this strange talk of "human beings" who are yet not "persons," beyond the word games and the straw men ... and beyond an insubstantial utilitarian ethic that fails to come up to the lowest levels of human justice.[11]

Pro-abortion rhetoric blasphemes the biological miracle of unborn life, casually passing it off as "a blob of tissue," "a clump of cells," or "just a growth, like a wart or a tumor." But Lewis Thomas suggests that a true understanding of human conception would utterly transform our thoughts about the fertilized human cell. He writes,

> The mere existence of that cell should be one of the greatest astonishments of the earth. People ought to be walking around all day, all through their waking hours, calling to each other in endless wonderment, talking of

nothing except that cell. . . . If anyone does succeed in explaining it within my lifetime, I will charter a skywriting airplane, maybe a whole fleet of them, and send them aloft to write one great exclamation point after another, around the whole sky, until all my money runs out.[12]

Abortion proponents picture the embryo or fetus as part of the mother's body, like an appendix. However, an unborn human being in the womb is a totally separate human being from the moment of conception: separate in genetic makeup, separate in blood type, and often separate in sex (in roughly half of all pregnancies, this supposed "part of a woman's body" is structurally and hormonally male). The blood of baby and mother never mix. Maternal and fetal blood vessels are so closely spaced in the placenta that oxygen, nutrients, and waste matter can be exchanged, yet these vessels never connect.

The separate personhood of the unborn individual is further demonstrated by the fact that the mother's immune system is triggered by pregnancy. Her body recognizes the embryo as a foreign invader, with its own elaborate and incompatible immune system, and begins a hormonal process of rejecting the baby, just as it would tend to reject a transplanted heart or kidney. In fact, it is this response of the mother's immune system that doctors generally use as an infallible indicator when testing for pregnancy.

Scientifically, then, the unborn are unquestionably separate persons, unquestionably human, unquestionably alive. It is this fact that has led several prominent early pro-abortionists to reverse themselves and become passionate defenders of unborn life. English physician Dr. Aleck Bourne was one of these. In the 1930s, Bourne was so committed to the pro-abortion cause that he publicized his illegal abortion practice for the purpose of provoking a trial to test the law—the celebrated 1938 case *Rex vs. Bourne*. Yet thirty years later, as an outspoken leader of the Society for the

Protection of the Unborn Child, Bourne was working to save lives he had once sought to abort. Bourne's heart was changed because his scientifically trained mind began to realize he had been taking human life.

Similarly, Dr. Bernard Nathanson, who was the director of the largest abortion clinic in America and a founding member of NARAL (the National Association for the Repeal of Abortion Laws; later the National Abortion Rights Action League), experienced a change of heart as the scientific facts surrounding abortion gradually became clear to him. In a 1974 article in the *New England Journal of Medicine*, Nathanson confessed, "I am deeply troubled by my own increasing certainty that I had in fact presided over 60,000 deaths." Nathanson came to this conclusion not on the basis of any religious beliefs (he is an atheist), but because of the scientific evidence.

Unfortunately, as George F. Will has observed, "science and society are out of sync." In contradiction to all the evidence, the United States Supreme Court has arbitrarily set the moment of birth as the legal boundary line for abortion. Clearly, however, birth is not the threshold of life, but merely a milestone on a journey that began some nine months earlier. Once a child is conceived, it's too late to say, "I don't want to bring a child into the world." A child is already in the world, unseen but here, just waiting to discover the world with new and eager eyes. The only choice left to us now is whether to accept that child or remove it from the world by violence.

The Sacred Body

Men go abroad to wonder at the height
of mountains, at the huge waves of
the sea, at the long courses of the
rivers, at the vast compass of the

ocean, at the circular motion of the
stars; and they pass by themselves
without wondering.

Saint Augustine

If anything is sacred the human body
is sacred.

Walt Whitman
I Sing the Body Electric

Do you not know that your body is
a temple of the Holy Spirit . . . ?

1 Corinthians 6:19

Over the years, as I've discussed the abortion issue with
many of my Christian friends, I've often heard comments
such as, "I wonder if we really ought to risk bringing conflict and division into the church over a secular issue like
abortion." At the same time, as Bernard Nathanson observes, "The pro-abortionists . . . seek to rule out discussion
of abortion in advance because it is a 'religious issue.'"[13]
Truly, the abortion question is both a secular and a religious
issue.

Yet the secular case for a pro-life ethic is compelling on
its own merits. As Nathanson concludes, the abortion question can be decided purely "on the biological evidence and
on fundamental humanitarian grounds, without resorting to
scriptures, revelations, creeds, hierarchical decrees, or belief
in God. Even if God does not exist, the fetus does."[14]

As Christians, we know that both God *and* the fetus exist.
Thus the compassionate pro-life ethic takes on a special
meaning for us as we begin to understand the biblical view
of human life. The clear pro-life truth of the Bible should
propel every Christian into meaningful action in the defense of all who cannot defend themselves. The Bible acti-
vates our conscience and inspires us to boldness and
commitment. As John Powell observes:

I have never understood how a minister of the Gospel could assure his congregation of God's love, and somehow not extend that love of God to the preborn. It seems to me that it would demand some kind of split in the personality to say to a congregation, "The good news is that God loves you!" and to say to the four thousand unborn who perish each day in our country, ". . . but not you. You see, you are not wanted." How does such a minister of the good news come face to face in prayer with the Lord who said, "Whatever you do to the least of my children . . ."?[15]

From the Bible, we know that unborn life is precious human life in the eyes of God. Psalm 139:13, 14, 16 says, "For you created my inmost being; you knit me together in my mother's womb. I praise you because I am fearfully and wonderfully made; . . . your eyes saw my unformed body. All the days ordained for me were written in your book before one of them came to be."

Similarly, in Jeremiah 1:5, the prophet hears God say to him, "Before I formed you in the womb I knew you, before you were born I set you apart. . . ." In Job 31:15, Job ponders the question of justice toward the last, the least, and the lowly: "Did not he who made me in the womb make them? Did not the same one form us both within our mothers?" Luke 1:15 describes John the Baptist as being filled with the Holy Spirit, even before he is born. And Paul, in Galatians 1:15, writes that God set him apart, even from his mother's womb.

Jesus, the Son of God, exemplified through His own life the special affection God has for children. In Matthew 19:14, He gathered them tenderly to Himself and said, "Let the little children come to me, and do not hinder them, for the kingdom of heaven belongs to such as these." And in Matthew 25:40, He said, "I tell you the truth, whatever you did for one of the least of these brothers of mine, you did for me." Thus, our love for Christ is demonstrated when we advocate the cause of the weak and defenseless—and there is no one more defenseless than an unborn child.

Yet there are some Christians who go to extraordinary lengths to avoid facing the contradiction between Scripture and abortion. I've even heard Christians wonder aloud if it wouldn't be better to abort a baby so that his soul might go straight to heaven, rather than bring him into a world of sin and suffering. This is not unlike the moral incoherency of the Anglican bishop who composed a prayer to be prayed on the occasion of an abortion:

> Heavenly Father, You are the giver of life,
> And You share with us the care of the life that is given.
> Into Your hands we commit in trust
> The developing life that we have cut short.
> Look in kindly judgment on the decision we have made
> And assure us in all our uncertainty
> That Your love for us can never change. Amen.[16]

The request that God "look in kindly judgment" upon the destruction of His creative work is incomprehensible—and the suggestion that we can turn killing into a sacrament, that we can somehow do the soul a favor by destroying the body, is an insult to reason and to the Scriptures.[17]

God is dynamically, intrinsically the author of life in the womb. He is intensely concerned for the welfare of children, born and unborn. Those who cut short these tender lives set themselves in direct opposition to God. If we fail to compassionately speak for those who cannot speak for themselves, then we have to confess that we, too, are in opposition to the plan of God. As Christ told the Pharisees in Matthew 12:30, ". . . He who does not gather with me scatters." Or, in other words, if we are not part of the solution, we are part of the problem.

We cannot put all the blame for abortion on society or the Supreme Court or the abortionists. As Curt Young pointedly observes, "Unborn children, handicapped newborns, and others are destroyed because the killing is permitted. I am not only speaking of the law here but of the refusal of citizens—including Christians—to take steps to curb the violence."[18] If we are honest with ourselves, we have to confess that abortion and other injustices exist not only because they are permitted by law, but because, to our shame, these injustices are tolerated by Christians.

All those who deny the unborn their personhood—the courts, the abortionists, and in our apathy even we ourselves—are like the lawyer in Luke 10 who asked Jesus, "Who is my neighbor?" This lawyer, observed Luke, "wanted to justify himself," so he asked the question everyone who wants to rationalize his guilt or apathy asks. Jesus' reply to this question was a story, the parable of the Good Samaritan, and it penetrated the lawyer's self-righteousness, just as it penetrates ours. The point of the story is that we are neighbors to all who are oppressed, beaten, stripped of rights, and threatened with death. *Neighbor* is an inclusive, not exclusive, term; it encompasses the entire human race.

Does our pro-life belief flow from genuine Christlike compassion, or is it merely a self-righteous pose? We answer that question whenever we honestly ask ourselves, "Who is my neighbor?" If we draw a line between ourselves and any other human being, as if to say, "This one is no neighbor to me," then our pro-life stance is just empty rhetoric.

The denial of neighbor status to a given class of people has masked all kinds of atrocities throughout human history. The enslavement of blacks in America was possible because they were deemed "three-fifths human" by the United States Constitution. European Jews of the 1940s were first deprived of their full status as persons by the Nazis before they were deprived of their lives. Over 1.5 million human beings are aborted each year in America because, according to a semantic contrivance, they have been deemed "unpersons." Oppression, injustice, and death have always been the lot of those who are not considered the neighbors of those in power.

Today, you and I have the power of life and death. We have a voice, a vote, a will, and the capacity to become involved in the fight for life. We who call ourselves pro-life readily acknowledge that an unborn child is a human life worthy of protection. But we have been less ready to recognize that the mother of that fetus is also a human life to be cherished and protected. She has problems and hurts and rights—not the moral right to abort her baby, certainly, but the right to have her needs considered along with the needs of her child. She is your neighbor and mine.

In fact, the lesson Jesus sought to teach us in the story of the Good Samaritan is that every individual in the world is our neighbor. Throughout our global neighborhood, many of our neighbors are being denied justice and life. Abortion takes 4,000 lives daily in America. Hunger kills 40,000 children a day in other parts of the world. And if an all-out nuclear war were unleashed, all the world's billions could be doomed in a single day. The numbers seem overwhelming, but the fact is that people die one at a time, and they can be saved one at a time.

True compassion dictates that we become committed to saving each life and all of life: the life of an unborn child threatened by abortion; the life of a woman with a crisis pregnancy who faces hard choices, alone and afraid; the life of a malnourished child who is dying amid the flies and the squalor of a parched African village; the life of a prisoner, condemned to years of degradation, cruelty, and homosexual rape; and the life that resides in the collective genetic heritage of the human race, now threatened by nuclear war.

In this chapter, we have just peeked behind the curtain that shrouds the mystery of human life, and there—in the coiled strand of DNA, in the developing structure of the unborn human individual, and in the words of Scripture—

we have caught just a glimpse of the enormous meaning of life. When a human being dies, whether born or unborn, the world may just lose one lone individual out of billions, but that individual loses the whole world. Justice and Christian compassion demand that we hold *every* human life to be irreplaceable and beyond price.

Whether a baby is aborted in America or starved to death in Africa, an enormous tragedy has taken place: A child has been cruelly denied the opportunity to discover his own meaning in the world. A precious gift of God has been squandered. Indeed, as John Powell has said, all life is a gift of God—and this gift must never be returned ungratefully and unopened. God's gift of life must be received into the world, and once received, it must be cherished.

Source Notes

1. An incident to illustrate just how sweeping the *Roe vs. Wade* decision was: In 1979, the *Chicago Sun-Times* ran a series of investigative stories on four Illinois abortion facilities, accusing them of being unsafe, unsterile abortion mills operated by elements of organized crime. Community organizations—including *pro-abortion* groups—demanded that the facilities be cleaned up or closed down. Yet, because 95 percent of the abortions were performed in the first trimester, government agencies were powerless to intervene. According to the Supreme Court, the state could not prohibit or regulate first-trimester abortions in any way.

2. For a more complete discussion of *Roe vs. Wade, see: Aborting America* by Bernard N. Nathanson with Richard N. Ostling (Garden City, N.Y.: Doubleday, 1979); *The Least of These* by Curt Young (Chicago: Moody Press, 1983); *A Private Choice: Abortion in America in the Seventies* by John T. Noonan, Jr. (New York: Free Press, 1979); and *Justice for the Unborn* by Randall J. Hekman (Ann Arbor: Servant Books, 1984).

3. Since *Roe vs. Wade,* most medical school graduates are no longer administered the traditional oath of Hippocrates. Instead, an oath composed by the World Health Organization of the United Nations is used. It contains no mention of abortion.

4. James T. Burtchaell, *Rachel Weeping* (New York: Harper & Row, 1982), pp. 249, 250.

5. Less than 2 percent of all abortions can legitimately be described as therapeutic or medically indicated according to a 1978 study by R. Illsley and M. Hall (*see Abortion in Psychosocial Perspective;* New York: Springer, 1978, pp. 11–32). Other studies suggest the figure may be less than 1 percent.

In a normal on-demand abortion, the doctor acts according to the choice rather than the medical interests of the patient. He performs essentially a social service, not a medical one; that is, his service is not *medically* therapeutic for the mother (much less for the fetus). A substantial number of women are, in fact, physically harmed by "safe and legal" abortions. Moreover, the physician rarely exercises his trained judgment as to whether or not the abortion is medically indicated, as he would in, say, the removal of a diseased appendix.

For centuries, medical ethics have forbidden the removal of healthy organs from patients. The idea that removing and destroying healthy fetuses is acceptable medical procedure is a quantum leap in the history of medical ideals. From a purely medical standpoint, the phrase "abortion-on-demand" makes exactly as much sense as "appendectomy-on-demand."

6. Peter Kreeft, *The Unaborted Socrates* (Downers Grove, Ill.: InterVarsity Press, 1983), pp. 71, 72.

7. From Isaac Asimov's foreword to *Enterprise* by Jerry Grey (New York: William Morrow & Co., 1979), p. 7.

8. Kreeft, *Socrates*, p. 62, 63.

9. Many people are surprised to learn that a fetus has respiration. Prior to birth, an unborn baby actually breathes amniotic fluid.

10. William A. Nolen, *The Baby in the Bottle* (New York: Coward, McCann & Geoghegan, Inc., 1978), pp. 231.

11. Bernard N. Nathanson with Richard N. Ostling, *Aborting America* (Garden City, N.Y.: Doubleday, 1979), p. 226.

12. Lewis Thomas, *The Medusa and the Snail* (New York: Viking Press, 1979), p. 155.

13. Nathanson with Ostling, *Aborting America*, p. 172.

14. Ibid., p. 176.

15. John Powell, *Abortion: The Silent Holocaust* (Allen, Tex.: Argus Communications, 1981), p. 102.

16. Quoted by National Catholic News Service, June 28, 1978.

17. Biblically, a human being is an indivisible whole expressed in three dimensions—a body/soul/spirit unity fashioned (as Genesis 1:26, 27 and 9:6 tells us) in the image of God. The triunity of human beings is expressed throughout the Scriptures, and notably in 1 Thessalonians 5:23: ". . . May your whole spirit, soul and body be kept blameless at the coming of our Lord Jesus Christ."

The word *spirit* (Greek: *pneuma*) appears to represent man's deepest inner self, the center of his awareness of God, and the truest "me-ness" of his being (*see also* 1 Corinthians 2:11). The word *soul* (Greek: *psuche*) appears to represent the seat of will, conscious thought, desire and emotion (*see also* Matthew 26:38).

Many Christians have the mistaken notion that the Scriptures disdain the body as a mere shell of dust housing our real selves, while elevating the spirit or soul. This idea views the real self as a kind of incorporeal animus, the spirit, which rises up and floats away from the ignoble body at death. This, however, is not a biblical idea but an ancient Greek idea, handed down from philosophers such as Plato, who in "Phaedrus" wrote, "We are contained within our bodies like an oyster within its shell."

Biblically, the life of the human spirit and the life of the human soul are welded inextricably to human biological life. First Corinthians 15:44 tells us that when the body dies, the grave takes possession of the *soma psuchikon*, the "soul-body." And when we are raised, as Jesus was raised on the first Easter, we will not be a kind of insubstantial floating spirit, as in Greek philosophy, but a *soma pneumatikon*, a "spirit body." Thus, the human body is not disdained but *exalted* by Scripture. The human body was created to be the temple of the Holy Spirit.

18. Curt Young, *The Least of These* (Chicago: Moody Press, 1983), p. 195.

Chapter Four

The Aborting of Truth

Lisa's Story

Not only do unborn children go
unprotected to the clinics, but
so do the mothers who carry them.
Curt Young
The Least of These

Shortly after my friend Mike Flavin joined our church staff as youth pastor in 1981, he and his wife Amy received a phone call from a young woman named Lisa. Her voice shaking and on the verge of tears, she explained that she desperately needed someone to talk to, and that someone from church had given her their number. Without hesitating, they invited her over.

Lisa arrived a few minutes later, and for the next two hours, Mike and Amy listened and counseled and prayed with her as she shared her hurt and confusion. She had been married for over two years, but now her marriage was in serious trouble. She was three or four months pregnant, and her body was just beginning to reveal her condition.

"Tom and I aren't getting along very well," she said. "There're a lot of bills, and we're really struggling financially. Tom says there's no way we can afford a baby right now, and he doesn't think we can stay together unless. . . ." She paused and began to cry, hugging herself as if to protect her unborn baby from some unseen threat. "He wants me to get an abortion," she continued, "then go live with my parents for a few months while he saves up some money. After that, he says we might get together again and try to make a go of our marriage."

"Have you already scheduled the abortion?" asked Amy.

"I'm supposed to be at the family planning center at 8:00 in the morning. They said they'd give me a prenatal exam first, then refer me to an abortion clinic."

"How are you going to pay for this?"

"I've got insurance."

"Is this what you want to do, Lisa?" asked Mike.

"I don't know. I don't want to lose this baby—but I don't want to lose Tom, either. Maybe if I have the abortion, Tom and I can work things out. I just don't know."

"Forget about what Tom wants for a moment and ask yourself what *you* really want. Do you really want to abort your baby?"

She thought for a moment, then looked up as if a profound realization had dawned. "No," she said firmly. "I want to keep my baby."

As they continued to talk with Lisa, it became clear to Mike and Amy that she was a thoughtful, caring young woman, but very dependent, passive, and prone to wishful thinking rather than decisive action about her own future. They encouraged Lisa to do what she deeply wanted to do: keep her baby, nurture it, and not compound her inner turmoil and her marital conflict with the regret and sorrow of an abortion.

They also talked with her about her need to commit her life to Jesus Christ. Opening the Scriptures, they shared with her about God's unconditional love for her and His ability to weave His perfect plan out of the tangled circumstances of her life. Finally, they promised to help her get the assistance she would need to continue her pregnancy.

Moved and encouraged by their compassionate concern for her, Lisa made a decision to commit her life to Jesus Christ. They knelt and prayed together on the living room floor. When they had finished praying, Lisa seemed to glow as she firmly announced, "I'm so glad I got to talk to you. I'm going to raise my baby to love Jesus, too."

"You've made the right decision," Amy told her, giving her a hug. "We'll have to keep praying that Tom comes to know Jesus, too."

"It must be a relief," said Mike, "to know you can get a little extra sleep in the morning."

"Oh, I still plan to keep my appointment at the family planning center," Lisa replied.

"Why?"

"I want to get my prenatal exam," she said. "It won't cost me anything, and it doesn't obligate me to have an abortion."

"I don't know, Lisa," said Mike. "I think you ought to stay away from that place. We could probably make arrangements with a doctor at our church to. . . ."

"Oh, that's not necessary. I'll be all right."

"Then let me go to the center with you," said Amy.

"No, really. I'll be fine," said Lisa. "I'll call you tomorrow when I get back home."

But by noon the next day, Lisa had not called, so Amy phoned her at home. As soon as Lisa answered the phone, Amy knew something was terribly wrong. "Lisa, what's happened?"

Lisa was sobbing. "After I had the exam, the doctor started to write out a referral for an abortion. I told him I'd changed my mind and I wanted to keep my baby. So he sent me to talk to a counselor. I told the counselor over and over that I wanted to keep my baby, but he kept asking me questions like, 'Do you know how much it costs to raise a child?' and 'How do you think a baby will affect your marriage right now?' Everything he said made so much sense. Finally, I just—*oh, Amy, I don't have my baby anymore. . . .*"

Lisa spent the rest of that day, and many others, unable to do anything but cry. Mike and Amy kept in touch with her over the next few months, but her depression never lifted. Her commitment to Christ apparently died along with her unborn child. Her marriage ended in divorce. Eventually she moved away, leaving no forwarding address. Mike and Amy have never heard from her since.

Lisa's story is far from an isolated case. A disturbing pattern emerges as you talk to women who have undergone the experience of abortion: It becomes clear that the practice of abortion is not so much a medical activity as it is an *industry*—clearly one of the most predatory and exploitative industries ever devised by the mind of man. The scramble for abortion profits leaves a trail of casualties in its wake: aborted human lives, aborted motherhood, aborted innocence, and significantly, aborted *truth*.

"Protected" From the Truth

Truth forever on the scaffold.
Wrong forever on the throne.
J.R. Lowell
The Present Crisis

Many people are under the mistaken impression that all abortion clients receive thorough, unbiased counseling before the procedure. In reality, the majority of abortion clinics seem to actively promote a climate of ignorance and passivity regarding the abortion experience. Sedatives are routinely given to anxious or hesitant patients soon after they are checked in, substituting a chemically induced serenity for any uncertainty they may be feeling.

Abortion patients are often told: "The fetus feels no pain," or, "It's just like the yolk of an egg," or, "It looks like a little ball of cotton." Most of those who work in abortion clinics know better than this, because (unlike their patients) they see the perfectly formed arms, legs, rib cages, and heads that are extracted in the abortion procedure.

The principal abortion clinic in the community where I recently pastored is part of a fourteen clinic chain that stretches up and down California, typical of a nationwide trend toward treating abortion as a franchise business, turning out aborted fetuses on an assembly line at prices from $185 to $2,500. Like most clinics nationwide, this clinic offers a free pregnancy test (in other businesses, this is called a loss leader, a product offered at a loss in order to attract business). After the pregnancy test, abortion counseling normally consists of the question, "Do you want to continue your pregnancy or terminate?" Or even, "When would you like to schedule your abortion?"

It's hard to escape the conclusion that consent ignorantly given is hardly consent at all. It doesn't seem unreasonable to expect abortion facilities to present their clients with the level of information doctors usually give a patient before, say, a gallbladder operation. A number of communities have enacted laws requiring informed consent, only to have them overturned by the courts. A typical informed consent law contains such provisions as:

- a requirement that patients be given accurate information regarding fetal development
- a requirement that patients be informed of the status of their pregnancy, the method of abortion that will be used, and the risks entailed
- a requirement that patients be informed of the availability of assistance and alternatives to abortion

- a requirement that unmarried patients below a given age obtain the consent of one parent
- a requirement that a one-day waiting period be observed before commencement of the abortion.

Pro-abortion organizations such as Planned Parenthood, the American Civil Liberties Union, and the National Abortion Rights Action League oppose even these most basic requirements of informed consent, claiming that they are judgmental and interfere with a woman's choice. The Supreme Court agrees, and has struck down these and many similar informed-consent provisions.

The pro-abortion forces seem amazingly blind to the illogic of their position. For example, the National Abortion Rights Action League condemns the requirement of a one-day cooling off period before abortions as an attempt to "frighten patients out of having an abortion," while at the same time calling for a nationwide thirty-day waiting period before sterilization to prevent women from being "coerced."[1]

Moreover, pro-abortion organizations paradoxically find themselves defending a demeaning view of women. The underlying assumption of their position would seem to be that a woman cannot be trusted to make rational decisions based upon all the information available. Instead, for her own good, she must be protected from the truth and prodded blindfolded into the abortorium.

Pro-abortion handbooks are also guilty of blurring the truth about abortion. One such book offers a sanitized and upbeat description of a suction abortion. A sampling: "Relax. . . . The amount of discomfort varies from none at all to something like bad menstrual cramps." Following the description of the procedure is a drawing labeled "A Vacuum Aspiration Abortion," a side view cross section of the female anatomy with the abortion instruments in place: the speculum holding the vagina open, the tenaculum clamped on the cervix, the cannula (suction tube) inserted into the uterus and touching a bean shaped, gauzy-looking object labeled "embryo." Unlike a real human embryo, this object has no face, no arms, no legs, and no personality. It is the perfect visual representation of the mythical "blob of tissue" pro-abortionists envision in the womb.[2]

Is this insult to feminine intelligence really necessary? Isn't a woman entitled to know exactly what it is she is aborting?

Proponents of abortion choice are often incensed by the so-called "bloody fetus posters" that anti-abortion protesters parade on signs in front of clinics. Granted, such posters may be in poor taste, but ugly as they are, they at least have the virtue of being accurate. As George F. Will observes, "People avoid correct words and object to accurate photographs because they are uneasy about saying and seeing what abortion is."[3]

Nor is it only women with unwanted pregnancies who are denied the truth. According to law, parents must be treated as the enemies of their pregnant teenage daughters; they are not entitled to know the truth. In most states, a pregnant girl as young as thirteen years old, who cannot even have her ears pierced without parental consent, can be removed from class, be provided with a one-day Medicare card, have her baby aborted, and be returned to school without her parents' knowledge. All decisions are made by a school counselor and a judge.

In the face of such laws and procedures, it's difficult to view our national abortion policy as anything but a kind of societal madness induced by the willful denial of truth and reason.

The Law vs. the Truth

Our government is the potent and omnipresent teacher. For good or

for ill, it teaches the whole people
by its example.
    Louis Brandeis
    Supreme Court Justice, 1928

When I interviewed my friend Laura for this book, one of the questions I asked her was, "If abortion had been illegal, wouldn't you have gotten an illegal abortion anyway?"

"No," she replied. "The choice was made easy for me because the Supreme Court said it was legal, it was sanctioned. To me that made abortion okay. The law allowed it, and it was an easy answer to a problem I had."

For many people, what is legal is the same as what is moral and true. When our laws become deranged, it's only natural that our society and its individuals begin to act in deranged ways as well. The horrors of Nazi Germany, for example, did not constitute a breakdown of law but of truth and conscience. The perpetrators of the Holocaust had followed the laws and edicts of the Nazi state, and in so doing they aborted the truth within themselves. When the butchers were convicted in the war-crimes trials at Nuremburg, it was not because they had broken the laws of Germany, but the laws of God.

Today in America, *Roe vs. Wade* has toppled a major barrier to barbarism. Our abortion laws are instructing a generation in a debased view of human life. Clearly, the Supreme Court's decision to legalize abortion did not force the killing of a single child; rather, it ripped the mask of humanity from the face of our society, revealing the naked and barely restrained animal beneath, an animal willing to kill for the sake of self-interest, profit, and private convenience. What was once punishable is now sanctioned. Killing is okay because the United States Supreme Court has said so.

Laws do not exist only for the purpose of punishing

harmful behavior. Laws also instruct—and it's important to remember that the word *instruct* comes from a Latin root word meaning "to join together or build up," the same root word from which we get the word *structure*. Laws give ethical and moral structure to our society. The law is the embodiment of a nation's social conscience and respect for human life and dignity.

It's not surprising to overhear a casual remark at a supermarket checkout such as, "I haven't told my husband yet. I'm waiting till I decide if I'm going to keep the baby or not." Nor is anyone shocked today to hear such social chatter as, "The parents give a baby life, and they have the right to take it away. It's the parents' choice whether a baby should be brought into the world or not." All around us we hear the *Roe vs. Wade* doctrines parroted in trite little nuggets of false folk wisdom:

"Abortion is a matter between a woman and her doctor."

"A woman has a right to control her own body."

"A baby's not a baby till it's born."

"Abortion is every woman's private choice. It says so right in the Constitution."

"What else are you going to do with all the babies nobody wants?"

Such statements are often summed up in one pious-sounding, well-worn cliché that seeks to render the whole issue of abortion law undiscussable: "You can't legislate morality." This slogan, however, doesn't hold up under thoughtful examination. The fact is that we have *always* legislated morality. Justice is a moral ideal, and it is the very purpose and function of our system of laws to establish enforceable norms of moral conduct. It is illegal to kill, steal, and rape because it is immoral to kill, steal, and rape.

The basic standard of morality in all such laws is the Golden Rule: "Do unto others as you would have them do unto you." Though best known in the form given by Christ in Matthew 7:12 or Luke 6:31, this golden standard of behavior is found in different forms among such diverse sources as Plato, Aristotle, Confucius, Hillel, the Book of Tobit, and the Hindu Mahabharata. The Golden Rule is a transcultural, transreligious ideal that enables us to put ourselves in the place of every other human being in the world. It calls us to treat all issues of life and justice as though we are looking through another person's eyes and living within another person's flesh. If we would not want to be killed, stolen from, or raped, then we must not kill, steal, or rape.

Logically, then, we must ask ourselves, "Would I have wanted to be aborted?" If the answer is no, then we must not abort others. Once we honestly face this intensely personal view of abortion and put ourselves in the place of an unborn human being; once we picture ourselves wriggling away from the vacuum tube that penetrates and devastates the only world we have ever known; once we mentally feel the tug of the suction, the snapping of our spine, the tearing of our limbs; once we consider the unutterable loss an unborn child suffers in being denied even a glimpse of the world he so briefly inhabited, abortion ceases to become an issue of statistics and polemics. It becomes the issue of a lone human soul in need of justice and protection. That is the instruction of the Golden Rule on the issue of abortion.

The cliché "you can't legislate morality" really means that in a pluralistic society, we should not prohibit *private* acts of immorality where no other person is injured. Applying this simplistic slogan to the issue of abortion, however, involves the demonstrably false assumption that the unborn are not persons. Abortion is not a matter of private morality, any more than murder, slavery, theft, abuse, assault, and exploitation are matters of private morality. Abortion is the unjust killing of human beings, and such injustice must be opposed in the arena of law and public policy. Justice demands that we defend the life and liberty of the unborn as we would any other class of human beings.

In the case of *Roe vs. Wade*, Justice Blackmun spoke for the court in stripping all rights and protections from the unborn, while explicitly denying any moral basis for his decision. Rejecting ethical truth and biological facts amassed over hundreds of years, Blackmun willfully refused to take a stand on the question of the personhood of the fetus. In fact, he denied that it was even necessary to take such a stand. Yet it is the job of a judge to decide justly, not expediently.

Is it just or unjust, right or wrong, moral or immoral, to kill the unborn? Blackmun only shrugs. That shrug is now the law of our land, instructing our society in the value of human life. The truth has been aborted in American law, and with it, the conscience of our nation.

The Propaganda War

> Our attempt to sort out the [abortion]
> problem is complicated by all-too-clear
> sloganeering, by sloppy use of medical
> data and terminology, and by the way
> in which perfectly functional words
> have become loaded through emotionalized
> usage in the political wars.
>
> Bernard N. Nathanson
> *Aborting America*

It has been said that the first casualty of war is truth. This is certainly true of the political war over abortion. The propaganda machinery on *both* sides is running at peak capacity, turning out steady streams of half-truth, near truth, untruth, and myth. The goal is to win the war, regardless of the price, regardless of the truth.

It seems to me that it makes no sense to be idealistically pro-life or idealistically pro-choice without at the same time being idealistically pro truth. We must embrace the truth, no matter what the cost. We must learn to carefully, attentively listen to the arguments and concerns of our opponents, even as we are seeking to uphold the truth of our own convictions.

Contrary to the melodramatic stereotypes on either hand, the average pro-life and pro-choice advocates are neither monsters nor closet Nazis. Both sides approach this issue with essentially humanitarian intentions. Both sides seek to do what is right (even though it's clear that both sides *can't* be right).

Obviously, there are many crass and venal abortionists who are interested in nothing more than the generous profits abortion offers. There may even be crass and venal anti-abortionists, for all I know (though I fail to see where there's any profit in it). But the fact is that the average person who feels strongly for or against abortion does so out of a sense of conscience and conviction. It's important that we recognize the conscience of our opponent and listen to his convictions, so we can respond sensitively and correct any errors in our own course of action.

If our sincerest goal is to help people in crisis and need, then we will genuinely seek to speak nothing but the truth. If, however, our goal is just to win the war and defeat the enemy, then our focus will inevitably be propaganda, not truth.

In 1985, Planned Parenthood Federation of America, Inc. (which receives much of its funding from the federal government) ran a series of full-page advertisements in *Time* magazine that were seemingly aimed more at defeating the pro-life "enemy" rather defending the truth. Among the sensational charges contained in these ads was the description of those with a pro-life conviction as an outspoken minority which engages in such tactics as harassment, physical intimidation, and clinic bombings. The reality, however, is that abortion has become an extremely divisive issue across

America, resulting in violence on *both* sides. For example, on Christmas Day 1984, three Florida abortion facilities were damaged by bombs and fire; no one was injured. Two young couples later confessed to the attacks, saying they had acted on religious convictions. Shortly after their arrest, arsonists set a fire in a church attended by one of the couples and spray painted "AN EYE FOR AN EYE" across the church doors.

It's all part of a familiar pattern: Violence spawns violence which spawns still more violence. It all begins with the legalized violence taking place within the clinics themselves. But does it make sense to hold an entire movement— either the pro-life or the pro-choice movement—responsible for the disordered actions of a few extremists on their fringes? Do such sensationalized accusations defend the truth—or destroy it?

Pro-abortion forces have long used deceptive measures of public opinion to bolster their position. In a 1981 address before the Winnipeg League for Life, Dr. Bernard Nathanson describes the tactics he observed as a founding member of NARAL, before his conversion to the pro-life movement:

> We fed the public a line of deceit, dishonesty, a fabrication of statistics and figures. We succeeded because the time was right and the news media cooperated. We sensationalized the effects of illegal abortions, and fabricated polls which indicated that 85 percent of the public favored unrestricted abortion, when we knew it was only 5 percent. We unashamedly lied, and yet our statements were quoted as though they had been written in law.[4]

Pro-abortion groups continue to use skewed or fabricated statistics to bolster their claim to speak for the majority. NARAL's Karen Mulhauser claims, "We are undisputed winners in the public opinion polls—we are the majority."[5]

And Eleanor Smeal, president of National Organization for Women, maintains, "81 percent of all Americans and 76 percent of all Catholics support the right of women to choose a safe and legal abortion."[6] The misleading suggestion behind such statements is that most Americans favor unrestricted abortion-on-demand.

An article in the May 1979 issue of *Redbook* magazine perfectly illustrates how objective data from opinion polls can be turned into wildly inaccurate statements about the public mind. *Redbook* commissioned the respected Gallup organization to conduct a poll on the question, "Do you think abortion should be legal under any circumstance, legal only under certain circumstances, or illegal in all circumstances?" The results:

Legal under any circumstance	26%
Legal under certain circumstances	54%
Illegal under any circumstances	17%
No opinion	3%

Redbook then added those first two figures together, 26 percent and 54 percent, and concluded that "the law of the land still accords with the will of the majority" since "80 percent of Americans say abortion should be legal under any or certain circumstances."[7] A moment's reflection, however, reveals that this conclusion doesn't fit the facts. The "law of the land" is actually unrestricted abortion-on-demand. Fully 98 percent of all abortions are on-demand abortions, not involving such circumstances as incest, rape, or therapeutic considerations. Adding the second and third figures together, 54 percent and 17 percent, reveals that 98 percent of all abortions performed in this country fall into a category which is *disapproved* by 71 percent of the public.

Of course, even if polls showed unanimous support for unrestricted abortion, that would not make abortion right; it would only make it popular. However, the truth is that abortion-on-demand is neither right nor popular, a fact that is adroitly disguised in pro-abortion propaganda. We will never arrive at just and truthful solutions to the life-and-death problems we face unless we begin to *speak* justly and truthfully. The issues are too urgent, and the cost in human life and suffering too dear, to be dealt with on a level of sensationalism, agitation, manipulated numbers, and tortured words.

Euphemy and Blasphemy

If we lose the meaning of words,
it is far more serious in practice
than losing our wealth or our
power. Without our words, we are
helpless and defenseless; their
misuse is our undoing.
>   Malcolm Muggeridge
>   *The End of Christendom*

Abortion. So confused are we
that even this term is fuzzy. On
operating room schedules, the pre-Blackmun
term that was written down was "therapeutic
abortion"; after Blackmun it became
"elective abortion." Now it is "termination
of pregnancy," the ultimate euphemism,
almost Huxleyan in its finesse.
To the gynecology residents, it
remains "scraping it out."
>   Bernard N. Nathanson
>   *Aborting America*

Truth cannot be understood apart from language. The ability to *think* in real terms depends on the ability to *speak* in real terms. The butchery of honest language is the butchery of truth.

Never in human history has sensible language been more seriously imperiled than it is today. Military strategists, for example, have developed their own "Strangelovian" language to translate unthinkable terror into an emotionless, methodical reality. Nuclear missiles are "birds" armed with "RVs" (reentry vehicles) which "dig out hard targets" in "surgical strikes," giving "a bad headache" to "the unfriendlies." Other branches of the government play similar word games to obscure rather than clarify their true meaning. One wag suggested this governmentese version of Benjamin Franklin's aphorism about death and taxes: "In this world, nothing is certain except negative biological function and revenue enhancement."

In similar ways, the practice of abortion has taken a heavy toll on the way people speak and think. For years, abortion practitioners have shied away from the word *abortion*, choosing instead the more sterile phrase "termination of pregnancy." Recently, however, even this arid term has begun to gather unpleasant associations in the public mind, so abortion clinics are increasingly beginning to refer to abortions simply as "treatments" or "procedures," or even "post-conception planning" or "menstrual extractions." The problem with euphemisms is that in time they often acquire the same connotation as the words they replaced, so that new and more meaningless terms must be devised to keep up the deception.

The fetus presents the greatest semantic problem of all. The object of an abortion, after all, is the destruction of the fetus, yet terms must be found that protect the mind of the patient (and often the mind of the abortionist himself) from awareness of this fact. In this book, I have tended to refer to the fetus as "the unborn child," "the unborn baby," or simply "the unborn," since the term *fetus* seems just too detached and clinical a word for the very personal individual increasingly revealed to us by medical science. The abortionist, however, must completely depersonalize the unborn in order to accommodate himself and his patient to the act of abortion.

The unborn are depersonalized by abortionists in two ways: euphemy and blasphemy. The word *euphemism* comes from a Greek root meaning "good speech"; similarly, the Greek root of *blasphemy* means "injurious speech." Some euphemisms for the fetus include "the conceptus," "fetal tissue," "the fetal-placental unit," "uterine cell matter," "the pregnancy," "the products of conception," or sometimes just "the P.O.C.s."

For some pro-abortionists, euphemisms fail to sufficiently neutralize the image of the fetus as a human being, so stronger and more hostile terms must be used. James Burtchaell lists some of the ugly anti-fetus nomenclature he has found in pro-abortion writings: "protoplasmic rubbish," "a gobbet of meat protruding from a human womb," "sub-human non-personhood," "so much garbage," "defective life," "a chunk of tissue," and "a parasite."[8]

Such abuse of language is not so much a conscious effort to deceive others as it is a tragic form of self-deception. It's an attempt to abort the truth from within. The people who use detached language regarding abortion are not necessarily bad people. Truly evil people can face the wickedness of their actions without flinching. It's the normal, so-called good people who need to hide from themselves the awful reality of the things they do.

The Nazi engineered Holocaust of World War II, for example, was not the work of Adolf Hitler alone, or even of the small handful of evil men surrounding him. It was carried out by thousands of good people—people who had been shopkeepers, farmers, lawyers, factory workers, bankers, and doctors before the war. They were people who just followed orders and did not think in real terms about what they were doing. In this, they are hardly distinguishable from those in our own country who tell themselves and others, "Whether abortion is right or wrong doesn't concern me. Abortion is legal, so I won't concern myself with the morality of it."

When you look closely at the lives of those who engineered the Holocaust, you don't readily find the familiar Nazi stereotypes of television melodrama. For example, Heinrich Himmler, chief of the dreaded SS, was a caring family man with a genuine fondness for children—except for the thousands of Jewish and Czech children he ordered murdered. Dr. Karl Brandt conducted hideous experiments on prisoners and developed some of the brutally efficient mass extermination procedures used in the death camps. Before the war, however, he had planned to go into medical missions work in Africa with Dr. Albert Schweitzer. Franz Stangl, commander of the Treblinka death camp, personally ordered the extermination of over a million people; yet, he was also a devout Catholic who regularly attended Mass, as well as a devoted husband and father to his wife and three daughters. His family insisted he was incapable of harming anyone.

The fact is that *every* human being is capable of enormous evil. We all have the ability to kill the truth within ourselves. The "good people" of Nazi Germany papered over acts of mass murder with words such as "resettlement," "special treatment," "disinfection," and "executive measures." The "good people" of America cover abortion with a verbal veneer of "terminations," "treatments," and "extractions." As James Burtchaell soberly observes, "The Holocaust spirit can be seen in our own country, our own people, our own time, our own mirror."[9]

It's time we begin to speak the truth about abortion, using real words with real meaning. Moreover, those of us who call ourselves Christians must begin to speak the truth *in love*, as Ephesians 4:15 tells us. Love calls us to listen carefully to others, to genuinely hear what they say, to consider their concerns, and then to speak truthfully, compassionately, and boldly—not to "slay the opposition" but to produce understanding, repentance, and healing.

The argument over abortion is basically asymmetrical. The two sides do not meet each other at common points of reference. Pro-life and pro-choice partisans might as well be shouting to each other from different planets. The pro-life advocate is essentially interested in the welfare of the unborn child. The pro-choice advocate is essentially interested in the welfare of the pregnant woman and doesn't even recognize an unborn child.

Even when both sides use the same words, they are speaking different languages. Take the word *life.* The opponent of abortion wants to save the biological life of the unborn child. He is pro-life. Yet the advocate of abortion choice hardly considers himself antilife. Rather, he talks about saving the life of the woman burdened by an unwanted pregnancy. Of course, he is not referring to a woman's biological life, but to her life-style. To continue a pregnancy is obviously not the same thing as to die. Still, the impact of an unwanted pregnancy on a woman's life is considerable, and there's a very real tendency among many pro-life people to discount this fact.

Or take the word *choice.* The advocate of abortion choice sees himself as a liberal, tolerant, reasonable person. He doesn't want to force his views on anyone. He just wants all people to be free to choose for themselves. The pro-life element, he believes, is composed of intolerant, sanctimonious meddlers who enjoy nothing more than interfering with the happiness of others. Yet he fails to recognize how horribly restrictive it is for the unborn individual to be killed in the womb and thus denied the *choice* of what to make of his own life.

I'm convinced that if we listen to one another, look at one another's evidence, and open our hearts to one another, we can begin to find many common truths. We can find compassionate and just solutions to difficult human problems. We can become *authentically* pro-life and *authentically* pro-choice. In Deuteronomy 30:19, God affirms the importance of both choice and life. "... I have set before you life and death, blessings and curses," He says. "Now choose life, so that you and your children might live. . . ."

Working together, understanding one another, people who love both life and the freedom to choose can find ways to care for the needs of women in crisis, families in crisis, and children in crisis. We can make the choice as a society to care and not to kill. Before such a time can ever come, we will have to learn to speak truthfully to one another and to dispel the myths that keep us apart.

Myth vs. Fact

> Rarely has an argument for a major
> social policy led the inquisitive
> so uncannily to its own disproof.
> James T. Burtchaell
> *Rachel Weeping*

Myth number 1: Opposition to legalized abortion is religiously motivated, and thus violates church/state separation.

Fact: According to this myth, people of religious conviction should be barred from speaking out on issues affecting public policy. As a result, our laws will be controlled solely by people without religious convictions. Under this peculiar view, Christians in Nazi Germany would have had no right or duty to oppose the Holocaust, nor would Christians of an earlier era have been able to oppose slavery.

The phrase "separation of church and state" is implicit in the First Amendment to the Constitution, though that particular wording doesn't actually appear in the amendment. People who cite the First Amendment or separation of church and state as ruling out Christian activism seldom quote the amendment, which reads:

> Congress shall make no law respecting an establishment of religion, or prohibiting the free exercise thereof, or abridging the freedom of speech, or of the press, or the right of the people to peaceably assemble, and to petition the government for a redress of grievances.

Clearly, the amendment was designed to protect activism, free speech, and the free exercise of religion. The framers of the amendment never intended to insulate government from the influence of religion, but to protect religion from the government.

Most pro-abortion literature is decidedly hostile to Christian faith. One pro-abortion author maligns religion as both tyrannical and sexist:

> Recognizing that religion has always been controlled by men who only recently have allowed a few women to become members of the clergy and to participate in formulating doctrine, many women question clerical rulings that do not show empathy for them. . . . With the capacity to experience the creation of human life within their own bodies, women instinctively feel that in matters of pregnancy they are more privy to the intent of the Creator than are male ministers, priests and rabbis.
> Today, as throughout history, religion restrains many of the faithful. But many women with unwanted pregnancies may prefer to negotiate religious beliefs on abortion directly with the Almighty rather than to chance the edicts of the clergy.[10]

Beyond the rather quaint notion that religion is a kind of all-male fraternity primarily interested in formulating doctrine and issuing edicts, there is in this statement—as in much pro-abortion literature—the undisguised suggestion that people are better off without religious faith.

In all of human history, there has been no more important force for the liberation of women than Christianity. It takes nothing more than a brief comparison between the treatment of women in Buddhist, Hindu, and Islamic cultures versus the treatment of women in the Christianized West to see what an enormous force for equality and justice the Christian faith truly is. In the Christian Church, as Galatians 3:28 says, there truly is "neither . . . male nor female, for you are all one in Christ Jesus."[11] And that is why we as Christians are called to an authentically profeminist ideal that seeks total equality for *all* people while carefully preserving that most awesome and miraculous of all feminine attributes, the ability to conceive and bring forth life.

Myth number 2: Opposition to legalized abortion is sexist, and an unjust infringement of a woman's right to reproductive freedom.

Fact: It is not the pro-life movement, but the abortion industry itself that represents a brutal and ruthless exploitation of women. Abortionists are almost exclusively men engaging in a highly lucrative business of destroying unborn life within their female patients. It's no accident that the pro-abortion cause is championed by *Playboy, Penthouse,* and *Hustler*—publications that have earned huge fortunes through the exploitation, depersonalization, and debasing of womanhood. Abortion is an enormous boon to men who subscribe to the *Playboy* philosophy of irresponsible sex. As feminist writer Juli Loesch caustically (but accurately) observes, most men view their responsibility in the wake of legalized abortion to be:

> To put up the cash for an abortion ("No hard feelings, okay?"); and if the man actually goes to the clinic with the woman—if he holds her hand—why, he's a prince. . . . And if the woman, for some reason, ends up having the baby after all, the man may feel perfectly justified in saying, ". . . I did my duty. I offered to abort it. Don't expect me to help support it."[12]

The oft-repeated demand by old guard feminists for "total reproductive freedom" is actually a demand for the freedom to be as sexually irresponsible as men often are. True feminism should be the celebration of the uniqueness of womanhood, not its denial. In recent years a new feminist consciousness has arisen to challenge the old feminist dogma that views women as oppressed victims of their own biology. Christian feminist Ann O'Donnell writes:

> How did it escape the notice of the old feminists that abortion is a convenience for everyone except the woman who undergoes "the procedure" and the baby that is destroyed? . . . How did it escape the notice of the old feminists that polls indicate women consistently oppose abortion more than men? Didn't they see the implications of the fact that the class most supportive of abortion is middle-class white males, the very group the old feminists maintain is responsible for the "oppression of women"? . . .
>
> The new feminist knows that her rights are congruous with those of the unborn child. Abortion is as much woman abuse as it is child abuse.[13]

And feminist writer Daphne du Jong views abortion as:

> Merely another way in which women are manipulated and degraded for male convenience and male profit. . . . Of all the things which are done to women to fit them into a society dominated by men, abortion is the most violent invasion of their physical and psychic integrity. It is a deeper and more destructive assault than rape.[14]

Clearly the act of abortion is an act of violence that leaves two casualties, one dead and one wounded. What's more, women are often coerced into the violent experience of abortion by boyfriends, parents, husbands, counselors, and even society, which has made abortion almost a duty for women with unplanned pregnancies. One of the most tragic and ironic aspects of the myth of abortion "choice" is that many women are made to feel that they really have no choice at all.

Myth number 3: Since millions of women will have abortions no matter what the law says, it is better to keep abortion safe and legal rather than return to the bad old days of dangerous "back alley"and "coat hanger" abortions.

Fact: The words *back alley* and *coat hanger* have come to symbolize the abortion climate prior to 1973. These terms suggests the sickening image of a desperate woman being mangled or murdered by a back alley butcher or inducing her own abortion (plus infection, mutilation, or death) by thrusting a straightened coat hanger or other object into her uterus. Pro-abortion propagandists often add vague or inflated statistics to this imagery. Typical is a recent national advertisement that spoke of huge numbers of women who underwent illegal abortions and the many whose health and lives were threatened. Such fictions have gained the force of conventional wisdom, and even of unassailable dogma, through years of repetition in the pro-abortion press and the general media.

A 1967 *New York Times* editorial, for instance, deplored the "pitiless restrictions throughout the nation which have resulted in more than a million illegal abortions and the needless death of four thousand mothers each year."[15] At about the same time, NARAL (then called the National Association for the Repeal of Abortion Laws) was claiming 5,000 to 10,000 deaths a year due to illegal abortions.[16] Actual statistics, compiled by the federal government from audited hospital and coroners' reports nationwide, showed 160 abortion related deaths in 1967 (by 1972, the year before *Roe vs. Wade*, the number had actually dropped to 39).

Authoritative studies by sex researcher Alfred Kinsey have shown that "back alley" and "coat hanger" abortions were rare in the days of illegal abortions. Kinsey found that

between 84 and 87 percent of illegal abortions were performed by qualified physicians, 8 to 10 percent were self-
induced, about only 5 to 6 percent were of the infamous
"back alley" sort. Thus, the average illegal abortionist in the
years before *Roe vs. Wade* was essentially indistinguishable
in training, procedures, and sanitation from the legal abortionists of today.

Still, there were clearly a number of deaths from botched
abortions (though orders of magnitude fewer than reported
in pro-abortion propaganda). The tragedy these statistics
represent should not be dismissed. Dr. Bernard Nathanson
states that it was the immense suffering he saw among victims of amateur abortions that initially led him to a pro-
abortion position. Would outlawing abortion, then, bring
about a return of the back alley and the coat hanger? No,
says Nathanson. If abortion were driven underground,
modern abortion technology would go underground with it.
Recently introduced drugs and equipment (such as the suction machine) would make black market abortion extremely
safe, while "do-it-yourself" abortions would be effected by
illicitly traded prostaglandin suppositories, not houseware.
"This may sound rather cynical," Nathanson concludes,
"but this is what would now happen in practice if abortion
were illegal."[17]

In an interview on "CBS Morning News" July 22, 1985,
National Organization for Women president Eleanor Smeal
invoked another fancied danger to women if abortion were
again illegal. "Can you imagine!" she exclaimed. "I mean, it
would be far worse than what happened when we tried to
outlaw liquor! Such a prohibition is unenforceable. There
are not jails enough to house the new criminal class of
women that this would create." Yet the fact is that laws re-
stricting abortion have always been directed at the *perpetrators* of abortion—the abortionists—not at the women who
are their victims.

The illegalization of abortion would not end the practice

of abortion, but it would seriously curb it, saving many lives. Moreover, the trivialized and debased view of human life that currently stains our national law and conscience would be replaced by a high ethical view, which would serve as a wise teacher to those making difficult moral choices.

Myth number 4: Legal abortion is a safe procedure.

Fact: Abortion is an invasive medical procedure which, like any other surgical procedure, entails risks of complication. The legalization of abortion has brought about a dramatic rise in the numbers of abortion-related complications. The Commission on Professional Hospital Activities in Ann Arbor, Michigan, reported that the rate of abortion-related complications treated in United States hospitals rose from 9,000 cases in 1969 to 17,000 in 1977.

So-called "safe and legal" abortion carries with it a 200 percent increase in the risk of miscarriage or premature birth in future pregnancies, 400 to 800 percent increase in the risk of ectopic pregnancies (pregnancy occurring in the fallopian tubes instead of the uterus), plus increased risks of loss of sexual response, increased guilt and psychological problems, and even suicide.[18] There is a 5 percent chance of sterility resulting from any abortion procedure.

In a suction abortion, the cervix, a tight ring of muscle at the base of the uterus that protects the fetus during pregnancy, is artificially forced open from the outside and clamped to permit the introduction of the suction tube. The muscles of the cervix can be torn, stretched, or irreversibly weakened so that future pregnancies cannot be held in place, increasing the chances of a later miscarriage or premature birth. The risk of such a complication is greatest with first-time pregnancies, and particularly among younger patients.

Perforation of the uterus can occur, leading to scarring and sterility. More rarely, the result can be the puncture of other organs, internal bleeding, or death. Surgery, even hysterectomy, is often required to correct a perforated uterus. Greater risk from this complication occurs when the procedure is performed under general anesthesia, because the uterus is softer and the patient cannot express pain when the injury occurs.

Infection is not uncommon in abortion, and is sometimes due to small parts of the destroyed fetus being left behind after a suction abortion. Infection can involve the uterus, the fallopian tubes, or the entire pelvic cavity. The result can be a painful, chronic condition called pelvic inflammatory disease (PID). Though PID can be caused by other factors than abortion, there is currently an epidemic of PID in this country, which is bringing about a dramatic increase in infertility nationwide. Legalized abortion is clearly the prime contributor to the PID and sterility epidemics now raging in America.

Myth number 5: Abortion is a necessary means to solve the problem of unwanted children.

Fact: There is no such thing as an unwanted baby. Infants that are unwanted by their parents are always wanted by someone else. Even in cases involving so-called "defective" babies, people willingly, eagerly come forward to offer such children a lifetime of love and nurturing.

The argument is sometimes advanced that it is cruel to bring unwanted children into the world, and that we do unwanted children a favor by aborting them. To this, Dr. William A. Nolen replies:

> Let us not pretend to ourselves that [abortion] is what the unwanted baby wants. I know, personally, hundreds of children and adults who were, before their births, unwanted. . . . Most of these unwanted children are now "wanted" by their parents. And even the few who may still be "unwanted" don't show any great desire to oblige their parents by committing suicide. Given a

choice, they, like most human beings, prefer life to death. The "unwanted" hang on to life as tenaciously as do the "wanted."[19]

During the last desperate throes of the Vietnam War, as the South Vietnamese army was collapsing before the assault of the Communist forces, an American C-5A cargo plane was loaded with orphaned Vietnamese children. These refugee children were scheduled to be evacuated to freedom in the United States. The heavily laden plane rumbled down the runway, lifted ponderously off the ground, lost power, and crashed. Scores of children were killed, injured or seriously burned.

One of those children, a little boy, was brought to the United States, where he received special medical attention and physical therapy for his injuries. He had been promised to an adoptive family in America, but when this family was told about the nature of his injuries, including the fact that he might grow up with a learning disability, they decided they were not equipped to cope with his special needs. Another couple stepped forward to accept and love this child: my friends, Jim and Sharon Patterson. Today at age thirteen, the Patterson's adopted son B.J. (short for Brian James) is growing into a tremendous, joyful, outgoing young man who loves people and who loves Jesus.

Today B.J. has a brother and sister. His little brother, Jason, was adopted through the county social service department. Jason's natural mother was an unwed teenager who had the courage to choose life and adoption for her child rather than today's more popular option of abortion.

B.J.'s little sister, Lindsay, was adopted privately. Her natural mother, a divorced woman in her late thirties, was told by the doctors to get an abortion. This woman courageously refused to kill the life within her, and through a series of amazing circumstances she made connection with Jim and Sharon. They spent some time with this woman toward the end of her pregnancy, getting to know her while sharing their dreams for Lindsay's future with her. They first saw their new adopted daughter just minutes after she was born. Soon afterward, Sharon gave this woman a gold ring Jim had bought to commemorate Lindsay's birth, asking her to keep the ring and present it to Lindsay someday when she was old enough to understand.

Each of these stories—B.J.'s, Jason's, and Lindsay's—is a beautiful story of love and acceptance, of a child who's life has been spared and given back to him. Every child can truly be a wanted child—no matter what his handicaps, his color, or the circumstances of his birth—if we commit ourselves to finding creative rather than destructive solutions to human problems.

Myth number 6: Abortion is a long-term solution to such social ills as overpopulation, poverty, and crime.

Fact: The notion that we can eliminate human problems by eliminating human beings is widespread, but false. Dr. Edward C. Allred, medical director for a chain of California abortion clinics, explains his involvement in the abortion industry:

> I really believe that [abortion] is essential as a matter of population control, as a matter of suppressing poverty, crime, all the other kinds of human problems that we have in our society. It's essential that we have this.[20]

This, in fact, is the principal motivation behind the pro-abortion movement. Justice Blackmun once stated his belief that abortion provided a cure for "the cancer of poverty."[21]

What most people fail to recognize is that the population control movement is essentially an elitist effort among wealthy, white, educated people to limit the reproduction of poor, nonwhite, uneducated people in this country and throughout the world. In *The Population Bomb*, the book that largely touched off the population-control mania in this country, Paul Ehrlich displays his open contempt for the world's poor:

> I came to understand the population explosion emotionally one stinking hot night in Delhi. . . . The streets seemed alive with people. People eating, people washing, people sleeping, people visiting, arguing, and screaming. People thrusting their hands through the taxi window, begging. People defecating and urinating. People clinging to buses. People herding animals. People, people, people.[22]

Population control literature drips with hostility for "the backward billions" who have created a "population plague" with their "untrammeled copulation." Such terms as "population bomb" and "population explosion" subliminally convey a connection between violence and human reproduction.

But is there a genuine population crisis in the world, leading to material shortages and famine? In *The Ultimate Resource*, Julian L. Simon documents the fact that food production per person around the globe has been *growing*, not diminishing, as the prophets of population doom would insist. In fact, statistics produced by both the United Nations and the United States Department of Agriculture conclusively demonstrate that the world's food supply shows a trend of steady improvement for as long as such statistics have been maintained (since 1948). Indeed, Simon ably demonstrates that one of the major causes for this improving trend is the *worldwide increase in population*.[23] Why, then, do we see such famine in places like Africa and the Indian subcontinent?

Having seen the devastation of hunger and malnutrition firsthand, I am convinced that the problem is not caused by too many people, but by circumstances of nature and climate combined with lack of education, governmental mismanagement, corporate and individual greed, and massive distribution problems. I have stood in remote African tribal villages that were once centers of starvation and suffering and have now been transformed into self-sufficient oases. Into these places, World Vision advisors have brought education and technical assistance to create ingenious irrigation and gardening projects. Where cultural practices and traditions allow, responsible family-planning information enables many families to choose the number of children to suit their needs and the available food supply. Having seen the success of these efforts, I believe that famine is not simply an accident of nature. With the knowledge and technology we have available to us, large-scale hunger is nothing short of a *crime* of indifference and neglect. Hunger is not a population problem, but a social, political, and spiritual problem.

In our own country in the late 1960s and early 1970s, scare peddling ads for the population control movement repeatedly warned, "The population bomb is still ticking." Well, the population bomb was a dud. The baby boom has become a baby bust. Yet population control groups blithely go about their misguided business, totally oblivious to the facts. The United States (like many other countries, including Italy, Japan, Sweden, West Germany, Finland, England, and Australia) has already passed the point of zero population growth and is now in a period of negative population growth. This is reflected in many ways, but perhaps most visibly in the ongoing crisis of the Social Security system. Social Security is having an enormous problem remaining solvent because we are not generating new taxpaying wage earners as rapidly as we are retiring old ones onto the Social Security rolls.

The United States government bestows millions on wasteful and deluded population control efforts (including abortion) through the State Department's Agency for International Development (AID), the World Bank, and various domestic programs. Julian Simon comments that AID "has publicly stated that the U.S. should act to reduce fertility worldwide for its own economic self-interest," and that the United States devotes millions "to reduce the fertility of the poor in the U.S." Simon concludes that the rationale for this policy is:

> It will keep additional poor people off the welfare rolls. Even were this to be proven—and as far as I know it has not been proven—is this in the spirit or tradition of America? Furthermore, there is statistical proof that the public birth-control clinics, which were first opened in large numbers in the southern states, were positioned to reduce fertility among blacks.[24]

Thus it is not surprising that many black leaders oppose abortion as white-imposed genocide against nonwhite races.

Clearly, the pro-abortion position must be rejected as elitist, prejudicial, antiminority, and antipoor. As Ella Grasso, the late governor of Connecticut once said, "Let us not kill the children of the poor, and then tell them how we have helped them."[25]

Myth number 7: The social cost of again outlawing abortion would be too high.

Fact: Pro-abortionists envision a world in which all problems can be cheaply disposed of and forgotten. Such a world does not exist. All actions have consequences, and these consequences cannot simply be inhaled into the bowels of a suction machine.

Some people argue that our society cannot afford the health care expense of the 1.5 million people who would have been born annually if not for abortion. Yet health care today consumes only about 8 percent of our gross national product—less than what we spend every year on movies, cigarettes, and alcoholic beverages.

Some people argue that our society cannot endure the sudden influx of "unwanted, meaningless lives" that would result from again outlawing abortion. Yet I believe we cannot afford to lose those lives, each of which is incalculably meaningful—not only in the eyes of God, but to the society of man. Every child conceived is a gift to the human race. If we nurture and guide that child, he will one day repay us a hundredfold, and he will invest a thousandfold into the next generation. But if we cruelly scrape him out of his mother's womb and immolate him on the altar of our selfishness and indifference, we rob ourselves of the contribution he would have yearned to make, if only we had let him live.

But beyond the wasteful human economics of abortion, there is the basic issue of justice for the unborn. We must begin by acknowledging that justice never comes without a price. This fact is proven by one of the saddest events of our nation's history. In order for black people to be freed from the yoke of white oppression in the mid-1800s, a price clearly had to be paid. Part of the price was economic: Slave owners had to forfeit the economic benefits of forced labor in order for human justice to be observed. Far more expensive, however, was the cost in human blood as soldiers on both sides of the Civil War paid the ultimate price for human freedom.

Justice for the unborn will be expensive, but we must be willing to pay the price. We must commit ourselves to winning the compassionate war for human life, and we must wage that war on every front: abortion, hunger, war and peace, prison reform, and on every other battlefield where human life is threatened. Once the battle for unborn life is won, we must join together to provide care and support for women who will no longer be permitted to abort their unplanned children. We must be willing to make every child truly a wanted child—not by destroying him, but by *receiving* him. We must be willing to use all the resources at our disposal in providing better health care, nutrition, education, and guidance for the generation that is to be spared from the abortionist's curette.

As James Burtchaell observes, "For justice to be done to another, fewer of the self's advantages can be preserved. There is no free justice."[26]

Source Notes

1. James T. Burtchaell, *Rachel Weeping* (New York: Harper & Row, 1982), p. 139.

2. Maria Corsaro and Carole Korzeniowsky, *A Woman's Guide to Safe Abortion* (New York: Holt, Rinehart and Winston, 1983), pp. 39–41.

3. George F. Will, "Discretionary Killing," *Newsweek* (September 20, 1976), p. 96.

4. John Powell, *Abortion: The Silent Holocaust* (Allen, Texas: Argus Communications, 1981), p. 75

5. Karen Mulhauser, Director's Report, NARAL *Newsletter* (August 1979) p. 3.

6. Burtchaell, *Rachel Weeping* p. 99.

7. Ibid., p. 100.

8. Ibid., p. 196.

9. Ibid., p. 195.

10. Myron K. Denney, *A Matter of Choice* (New York: Simon & Schuster, 1983), p. 113.

11. For a more thorough discussion of the scriptural case for the liberation and equality of women in society and in the Church, see *Chauvinist or Feminist? Paul's View of Women* by Richard and Joyce Boldrey (Grand Rapids: Baker Book House, 1976), and *The Apostle Paul and Women in the Church* by Don Williams (Van Nuys: BIM Publishing Co., 1977).

12. Burtchaell, *Rachel Weeping*, p. 131.

13. Ann O'Donnell, "Why I'm Pro-Life: A Feminist Approach," *Life Cycle* (Spring 1984), pp. 6, 7.

14. Burtchaell, *Rachel Weeping*, p. 131.

15. *The New York Times* (April 29, 1967), p. 34.

16. Bernard N. Nathanson with Richard N. Ostling, *Aborting America* (Garden City, N.Y.: Doubleday, 1979), p. 193.

17. Ibid., pp. 193, 194.

18. Suicide statistics belie the notion that abortion is therapeutic for women in emotional or mental crisis. The suicide rate is actually higher among recent abortees than among the general population; among women who have recently given birth, suicide rates are lower than for the general population.

19. William A. Nolen, *The Baby in the Bottle* (New York: Coward, McCann & Geoghegan, 1978), p. 227.

20. From the film *A Matter of Choice*, distributed by New Liberty Enterprises, 1980.

21. Burtchaell, *Rachel Weeping*, p. 259.

22. Paul Ehrlich, *The Population Bomb* (New York: Ballantine Books, 1968), p. 15.

23. Julian Simon, *The Ultimate Resource* (Princeton: Princeton University Press, 1981); see esp. pp. 54–69. This book convincingly documents the case that, contrary to conventional wisdom, the world is not approaching a genuine crisis in regard to population and limited resources. Simon began his research as an advocate of population control, but became convinced by his research that the population scare had been seriously overstated by people and organizations that were either misguided or who had an economic or political interest in controlling the reproduction of the world's poor and nonwhite peoples.

24. Ibid., pp. 7, 8.

25. Powell, *Abortion*, p. 117.

26. Burtchaell, *Rachel Weeping*, p. 287.

Chapter Five

The Aborting of Love

A Death in Bloomington

Rescue those being led away to death;
hold back those staggering toward
slaughter. If you say, "But we knew
nothing about this," does not he
who weighs the heart perceive it?
Does not he who guards your life know
it? Will he not repay each person
according to what he has done?

Proverbs 24:11, 12

I believe that each newborn child
arrives on earth with a message
to deliver to mankind. Clenched in
his little fist is some particle
of yet unrevealed truth, some missing
clue, which may solve the enigma
of man's destiny. He has a limited
amount of time to fulfill his mission
and he will never get a second chance
—nor will we. He may be our last hope.
He must be treated as top-sacred.

Sam Levenson
Everything But Money

The baby was christened by a court of law. Perhaps his mother and father gave him a name of their own choosing, perhaps not. But to the world this child became known as Baby Doe.

He was born in Bloomington, Indiana, on April 9, 1982, with a condition called Down's Syndrome. Baby Doe also had a malformed esophagus that made breathing difficult and taking nourishment impossible. The parents' family doctor and a consulting pediatrician both agreed that the esophageal problem could be easily corrected by surgical means; indeed if it was not corrected, the child would die from the effects of starvation combined with the deadly regurgitation of digestive juices from the stomach into the lungs. The resulting "chemical pneumonia" would cause the baby's lungs to be digested and destroyed by stomach acid.

How serious were the child's deformities? The operation to correct the esophagus is a fairly common procedure with a 90 percent success rate. The only other handicap this baby boy had was Down's Syndrome itself, resulting from an extra chromosome in his genetic code. Though Down's Syndrome babies generally grow up retarded and somewhat handicapped, some reach near normal intellectual capacity by adulthood, and only a small percentage could be termed severely retarded. There is no way to know at birth what a baby's intellectual capacity is. One of the nurses who attended him later recalled, "He'd open his eyes when I stroked his head. He looked like a perfectly normal little boy. Yes, he did have the eyes of a Down's child, but other than that he looked normal."[1]

Baby Doe was in no immediate danger, had no truly crippling malformations, and could reasonably be expected to live as long, normal, and happy a life as any Down's Syndrome child. The "Doe" family doctor and the pediatrician recommended the baby be transferred to a nearby children's hospital for immediate surgery. But the obstetrician who delivered the baby countered their advice with another suggestion: The parents could simply refuse consent for the surgery and let the child die of starvation and pneumonia. The parents of Baby Doe, who didn't want a handicapped baby, took the obstetrician's advice.

Over the strong protests of the other two physicians, the obstetrician ordered the baby placed in the special-care nursery. His orders were taped to the incubator: The baby was not to be fed intravenously, but the nurses could feed the child orally "if desired," though it was noted that oral feedings would likely result in death. It was a strange order, since the doctor knew that oral feedings would never pass the closed esophagus and would probably choke the infant. The doctor also ordered the child kept "comfortable" and sedated (though one of the nurses on the case later stated that this order was as much to silence the baby's pitiful cries as to keep him comfortable).

This was just the beginning of a swirl of events that eventually focused the attention of the nation on the suffering of one child. On April 10, hospital administrators, concerned that this case could expose the hospital to criminal liability, obtained a judicial hearing to determine whether the parents of Baby Doe had the right to deny him basic medical attention and food. The Superior Court judge sided with the parents and against their newborn son.

The next day, April 11, the nurses in the special-care nursery rebelled. Forced to work around a baby who was being deliberately and slowly killed, these nurses found it almost impossible to do the job they were trained for and devoted to: giving care and life to children who needed special nurturing. Hospital administrators sought to placate the nurses by transferring the baby to a private room. This transferred the problem to other nurses, who were required

to give the dying baby injections of morphine and pheno-
barbital to keep him tranquilized.

The story of Baby Doe headlined newspapers and television news programs across the country. Over a dozen people came forward, offering—even pleading—to adopt Baby
Doe and assume all the expenses for the surgery to save his
life. The parents refused.

By April 13, Baby Doe was a shrunken and gaunt appari-
tion with parched, blackened lips and protruding ribs. He
fought hard for life, straining for breath while his lungs
were being eaten away by gastric juices. Three times his
breathing stopped for as much as a full minute, then started
again as he struggled to live. Blood began to pour from his
mouth and nose. One of the nurses whose job it was to keep
him sedated later recalled, "It was the most inhumane thing
I've ever been involved in. I had all this guilt, just standing
by, giving him injections and doing nothing for him. . . . I
couldn't sleep for a long time afterwards. Every time I
closed my eyes, I'd see that baby lying there bleeding and
fighting for breath."[2]

At 10:01 P.M. on April 13, after six days of intense suffering, starving, and struggling vainly for life, condemned to
death for the crime of being unwanted, Baby Doe died. An
autopsy showed no physical impairments except a single
easily treatable defect in his esophagus. In America, in the
1980s, a child was deliberately put to death because he was
born retarded.

Silent Cries for Love

> It used to be easy to know what
> we wanted for our children, and now
> the best for our children might mean
> deciding which ones to kill. We've
> always wanted the best for our

grandparents, and now that might
mean killing them.
>> Dr. William Gaylin
>> Columbia University

A fierce-looking nation without
respect for the old or pity for the young.
>> Deuteronomy 28:50

For all the media attention it received, the death of Baby Doe was far from an isolated case, even in 1982. Some physicians had openly admitted their participation in infanticide cases for over a decade by the time Baby Doe was starved to death. As early as January 1972, an article appeared in the *New York Times Magazine* describing the practice of infanticide upon Down's Syndrome children at the University of Virginia Medical Center.

Then in an October 1973 article in the *New England Journal of Medicine*, Dr. Raymond S. Duff and Dr. A. G. M. Campbell of the department of pediatrics, Yale University School of Medicine, reported on a study they had completed on 299 infant deaths that had occurred in an eighteen-month period at Yale-New Haven Hospital. They found that 14 percent of these deaths—43 children—occurred because medical personnel deliberately withheld or withdrew basic treatment. The reason Duff and Campbell published this article was not to expose the practice of killing "defective" newborns, but to advocate it.

Duff and Campbell suggested that, since it is unlikely that parents would come to a physician and ask him to end their child's life, it was incumbent upon the physician to tactfully guide the distraught parents of a retarded or severely handicapped child to a decision to let the child die. Thus the parents would be relieved of the "seemingly pointless, crushing burdens" that would accompany caring for a handicapped child.

This is not to say that we are morally obligated to prolong the death process of a child that is obviously born dying. But it's important to understand that Duff and Campbell were not talking about withholding extraordinary and heroic medical measures from obviously doomed children. The forty-three infants in the Yale-New Haven study were not dying; they had *treatable* defects, but treatment was deliberately withheld because it was felt that their continued existence would be a heavy burden on their parents and society. "We recognize," they admitted, "great variability and often much uncertainity in prognoses and in family capacities to deal with defective newborn infants. . . . Prognosis was not always exact and a few children with extensive care might live for months and occasionally years. Some might survive and function satisfactorily." Nevertheless, Duff and Campbell were willing to prescribe death as a "management option" for viable handicapped infants, and this lethal prescription was based not on medical considerations but on such criteria as social convenience and their subjective (and largely unreliable) estimates of the infants' future "quality of life."

The public statements of Duff and Campbell led to several investigations in the press, as well as a series of hearings in 1982, conducted by the Connecticut State Senate Public Health Subcommittee. The investigations uncovered more cases of infanticide, including one case in which a Down's baby was starved to death over a period of twenty-three days. The situation at Yale-New Haven is unique only in that the doctors reported on their own activities in the *New England Journal of Medicine*. Without the doctors' own bold admission and advocacy of infanticide, these deaths would have taken place quietly and in secret.

No one knows how many cases of infanticide occur per year in America. It could be hundreds, or it could be thousands. Occasionally an infanticide case makes the headlines; most, by far, do not. Victims of infanticide are buried on paper before they are buried in the ground. Baby Doe's autopsy report, for example, did not say, "Death due to deliberate starvation and withholding of medical treatment." It said, "Cause of death: chemical pneumonia," and the county coroner ruled the death as being due to natural causes. The Baby Doe case would have been quietly disposed of if conscientious doctors and nurses hadn't protested and if worried hospital administrators hadn't brought the matter before the court.

Many other Baby Does are going quietly to their fate, their cries for life and love silenced by heavy infusions of drugs. Melinda Delahoyde, a pro-life advocate and the mother of a Down's Syndrome child, notes:

> Events do not happen in a vacuum; infanticide did not just suddenly appear on the American scene. Ideas have consequences, and ideas about the low value of human life took root in our culture long before Infant Doe was killed in Bloomington. Infanticide is the logical conclusion of a mind-set that casually allows the destruction of more than 1.5 million unborn children every year.
> Abortion leads to infanticide.[3]

The killing of newborns was the first fatal step beyond killing the unborn, legalized by judicial fiat in 1973. Now what about the next step? If Baby Doe can be put to death simply because he is unwanted, can Grandma and Grandpa Doe be far behind?

In *The Baby in the Bottle*, Dr. William A. Nolen warns:

> Why, if we are willing to kill healthy, young fetuses, should we not be willing—even eager—to kill those whose lives are not only a burden on society but seem to us—if not to them—hardly worth living? The proabortionists are understandably reluctant to admit it, but the step from liberal abortion to euthanasia is a perfectly logical one. . . .

We have only to consider the atrocities of which "civilized" people have been guilty in the last fifty years to realize that we are not as incapable of barbaric behavior as we would like to believe. Casual acceptance of abortion as an answer to social problems could, if we are not careful, be the first step down a path that leads to the end of civilization as we know it.[4]

Dr. Nolen's warning may have seemed dire and far-fetched to his readers in 1978. Today, it's not difficult to believe that the end of civilization is already in view.

The Vanishing Child

> But what am I?
> An infant crying in the night,
> An infant crying for the light,
> And with no language but a cry.
> Alfred, Lord Tennyson
> *In Memoriam A.H.H.*

Prior to 1973, adoption agencies used to advertise the need for more adoptive parents. But if you or an acquaintance has sought to adopt a child in recent years, you know what a dramatic change has taken place. Adoption agencies now place prospective parents on waiting lists for three, four, five, or more years. Such bizarre social phenomena as the black market baby trade and surrogate motherhood have become almost commonplace.

There is only one reason for this sudden turnabout: The babies that would have been adopted before *Roe vs. Wade* are simply aborted now. We are witnessing the silent disappearance of 1.5 million adoptable children every year.

Before *Roe vs. Wade*, adoption was by far the principal means of dealing with an unwanted pregnancy. There are hardly any reasons for aborting a baby that are not equally good reasons for giving the baby up for adoption. Why, then, do 1.5 million women choose to abort their children instead of giving them life and a chance for love in a family that deeply desires a child? Reasons given by women who choose abortion over adoption seem, at best, murky and incoherent.

Katrina Maxtone-Graham's book *Pregnant by Mistake* contains interviews with seventeen women who obtained legal abortions in New York (which legalized abortion-on-demand in 1970). Asked why they chose abortion over adoption, most of these women inexplicably seemed to regard adoption as an unthinkably horrible suggestion. One woman in her early twenties said, "You would wonder all your life, every [time you saw a] little child, 'I wonder if that's mine.' 'What would he or she be like now?' I don't believe that I could ever have a child and give it up. I could have an abortion and forget that, much easier than I could have a child and give it up."[5]

"To have unmarried girls go through with it and then give it up for adoption; how—how can you be so cruel?" said another.[6]

"I don't think you have any right at all to create a human being and *give it away*. That is not your job in life," responded another.[7]

"Oh my God! I couldn't even consider that!" exclaims another. "I feel as a *woman* that [adoption is] absolutely unfair and ludicrous. I think at times there are real reasons for a woman not to keep a child, but then she shouldn't have *had* it. She should have had an *abortion!*"[8] Strangely, the women in these interviews see adoption as somehow cruel while demonstrating no discernable remorse about the destruction of the unborn child.

James T. Burtchaell suggests that the reason so many women now prefer abortion to adoption is that selfish, possessive love has replaced unconditional love in our cultural attitude toward maternal fulfillment. Terming this view a "Raggedy Ann attitude towards children," he explains,

> It is interesting to analyze the women's understanding of "wanting a child." It seems a proprietary thing: to possess, to be satisfied with, to have. There is only a faint notion of joining one's life to another human being, of accommodating, being prepared to rearrange one's preferences for the sake of another. . . . Women who reject adoption as either hurtful to their offspring or hurtful to themselves reveal in their remarks this tendency to consider children as proprietary objects. They are desired or annulled as the mother wishes, very much to suit her plans and needs.[9]

This growing cultural attitude of self-centered possessiveness toward children, which has already produced some 18 million abortions since 1973, may also explain the eerily precise correlation between abortion and child abuse statistics. The United States Children's Bureau estimated that about 60,000 incidents of child abuse occurred in 1972, the year before *Roe vs. Wade*. This figure was tragic enough, but then came an *explosion* in child abuse statistics. By 1976, reported cases numbered 413,000 (a 588 percent increase in just 4 years), according to an American Humane Association study. By 1981, the numbers topped 851,000 (a 1,318 percent increase over 1972). Today, the statistics continue to compound at a rate of 12 percent to 15 percent every year.

Statistics reflect only known cases of child abuse. As *Time* writer Ed Magnuson noted in a report on the subject, "only a small fraction of all abuses is reported. Guesses on the 'tip of the iceberg' range from 10 percent to 25 percent of actual cases, but no one really knows."[10] Though the statistics show an unmistakable and dramatic upsurge of violence against children *precisely coinciding* with the nationwide legalization of abortion, some pro-abortionists discount any connection, saying that it is not actual violence but the reporting of violence that is on the upswing. Yet no one knows of any change in the method of uncovering and tabulating crimes against children that would result in figures that increase not just incrementally but by astounding orders of magnitude.

Advocates for abortion have long invoked the heartbreaking tragedy of child abuse as a justification for unrestricted abortion. The rationale is that children who are unwanted at conception grow to be resented and abused in childhood—hence, Planned Parenthood's famous slogan, "Every child a wanted child" (with its unspoken suggestion that every *unwanted* child should be destroyed). There is even a kind of superficial logic in the assumption that "unwantedness" leads directly to abuse. This assumption, however, is betrayed by the facts.

According to authoritative studies conducted by pediatrician E. F. Lenoski at the University of Southern California Medical School, more than 90 percent of abused children are wanted children; a matched control group of nonabused children showed only 63 percent were wanted or planned pregnancies. Contrary to stereotype and widely held assumptions, battered children tend to be of planned, legitimate birth, born to mothers who have expressed full satisfaction with the circumstances of their pregnancies.

Noted child abuse researcher C. Henry Kempe, who coined the term "battered-child syndrome," identifies what he sees as the basic cause of child abuse: parents who want children—but for the wrong reasons. "Basic in the abuser's attitude toward infants," he concludes, "is the conviction, largely unconscious, that children exist in order to satisfy parental needs." Notice that this is also the principal reason parents abort children: They see the child that has been conceived conflicting with the needs they wish to satisfy. So it is not hard to see how the same self-centered attitude toward children leads both to abortion and abuse.

Other clinical studies are uncovering additional psychological and behavioral links between the motive to abort and the motive to abuse. One 1980 study of the abortion/abuse connection, conducted by Canadian psychiatrist Philip G. Ney, found: (1) that Canadian provinces with high or low abortion rates had correspondingly high or low rates of child abuse; (2) that the increase in child deaths due to abuse coincided with the increase in numbers of abortions; and (3) that women who abused their children had higher abortion rates than the general population. "Having to treat so many battered children," he concluded, "I began to worry that using abortion to make every child a wanted child might be backfiring. When I examined the evidence, I became convinced that most of the abused children resulted from wanted pregnancies and that elective abortion is an important cause of child abuse." Ney went on to explore some possible causes for the abortion/abuse correlation he found:

> Having an abortion can interfere with a mother's ability to restrain her anger toward those depending on her care. Abortion might also weaken a social taboo against harming those who are defenseless. . . . An aborting person, having already repressed her instinctive caring for her unborn young, might be less inhibited in giving vent to her rage at a whimpering child. . . .
>
> Abortion also lowers women's self-esteem and there are studies reporting a major loss of self-esteem in battering parents.[11]

And in another medical journal, Ney observed,

> The mother's guilt or high expectations may be reasons why there is this high correlation [between abortion and child abuse]. A more plausible cause is that because of guilt, there is antepartum depression that in-

terferes with the mother's ability to bond. Children not
well bonded appear to be at higher risk to a parent's oc-
casional rage or neglect.[12]

Ever since 1973, unwanted children have been aborted
with increasing abandon, and thus it would seem reasonable that—with some 18 million fewer children alive today
than would have been the case without legal abortion—we
should see a major drop in the numbers of abused children
instead of the over 1,000 percent increase we have seen. As
Bernard Nathanson observes, "If anything, the statistical reports would lead one to conclude that liberal abortion laws,
not strict ones, foster child abuse."[13]

One authority on the mistreatment of children, Dr. Vincent J. Fontana, argues persuasively against abortion as a
solution to the child abuse problem:

> In search of a quick and easy solution to the ugly real-
> ity of child abuse, a great many people have come up
> with glib answers. . . . Abortion is the favorite theme of
> the moment. The thrust of the argument is, of course,
> toward the prevention of child battering, neglect, and
> abuse through the prevention of children. This method
> of solving the maltreatment problem would also have
> the virtue of giving us fewer children with chickenpox,
> fewer children with measles, fewer children with men-
> ingitis, fewer children to get knocked down by automo-
> biles, fewer children to fall out of trees, fewer children
> to skin their knees in the playground, fewer children to
> grow up well and strong and loved. There would be
> fewer children and, therefore, fewer problems all round.
> It might be a wonderfully neat solution, if it were not
> quite so sweeping and simplistic, or if it were only
> valid.[14]

Clearly, we are witnessing not only the abortion of 1.5
million children every year, but the abortion of *love*. In act

after deadly act of abortion, over 4,000 times every day, mother love is destroyed and replaced by guilt and self-hatred. Thousands of would-be adoptive couples are denied the opportunity to give life and love to a child. Moreover, abortion sends a chilling message to millions of children, for as Curt Young has said, "The widespread acceptance of abortion conveys to all children the frightening message that the love they receive is conditional."

The Planned Parenthood slogan, "Every child a wanted child," is an admirable goal. But we have to ask ourselves if the way to achieve that goal is by destroying unwanted children or by teaching parents to want and love their children unconditionally. Stanley Hauerwas cogently states the difference between the world's view of the child and the Christian view:

> From the world's perspective, the birth of a child represents but another drain on our material and psychological resources: children, after all, take up much of the energy that we could use in making the world a better place. . . . But from the Christian perspective, the birth of a child represents nothing less than our commitment that God will not have this world "bettered" through the destruction of life.[15]

The only way to truly better the world is to live after the example of Jesus Christ, who said, "Let the little children come to me, and do not hinder them, for the kingdom of heaven belongs to such as these" (Matthew 19:14).

Even when a pregnancy is not wanted, that child can find acceptance and unconditional love as the child's mother is compassionately supported by Christians while she decides whether to keep or give up her baby; as she is showered with maternity and baby clothing and other necessities; as she is given a place to live, a place to work, and a place of acceptance and encouragement; as the child in need of a home is given a place of belonging, regardless of the circumstances of his birth, the color of his skin, or his hand-icaps.

The Greatest Quality of Life

I believe there is no life so degraded,
deteriorated, debased, or impoverished
that it does not deserve respect and
is not worth defending with zeal and
conviction. . . . It is an honor for
a society to desire the expensive
luxury of sustaining life for its
useless, incompetent, and incurably
ill members; I would almost measure
a society's degree of civilization
by the amount of effort and vigilance
it imposes on itself out of pure
respect of life.

> Jean Rostand
> French biologist-philosopher

I served as eyes for the blind and feet
for the lame. I was as a father to
the poor. . . . I knocked out the fangs
of the godless oppressors and made
them drop their victims.

> Job 29:15–17 TLB

Abortion is prescribed as a cure for defective children on the grounds that eliminating the burdensome members of our society preserves something called quality of life. This so-called quality is variously defined by different people. For some, it refers to the quality of life-style that the handicapped person could himself expect to experience. The argument goes that a person with severe handicaps is trapped in a life not worth living, so he would be better off dead than living a life with so little quality.

Others see the quality of life issue in terms of the quality of life-style that the handicapped person's family must endure. The handicapped person is such a burden (so this reasoning goes) that the family is better off if the burdensome person could somehow be disposed of.

Still others view quality of life in terms of a standard of quality that human beings should measure up to, both physically and mentally. A low-quality life (says this view) should be terminated, lest it become a burden on society. This is pure survival of the fittest ethics, with the least fit being consigned to the ash heap.

Attorney Glanville Williams goes so far as to suggest that merely allowing handicapped babies to live is an "offence to society." He writes, "To allow the breeding of these defectives is a horrible evil, far worse than any that may be found in abortion."[16] Handicapped people are understandably dismayed that such arguments are currently gaining acceptance.

The Christian view of human life does not allow people to be evaluated on a quality-of-life basis, regardless of how it is defined. Psalm 82:3,4 tells us that God is on the side of the weak and fatherless, the needy and oppressed; Psalm 72:13,14 says, "He will take pity on the weak and needy and save the needy from death. He will rescue them from oppression and violence, for precious is their blood in his sight." First Corinthians 12:22–26 says that those among us who are weaker are actually indispensible; those who seem less honorable should be treated with special honor; if one person suffers, we all suffer. The Christian world view does not permit any human life—regardless of being "unwanted" or "defective" or "burdensome"—to be sacrificed according to some notion of quality of life.

The only quality of life recognized in the Christian Scriptures is the life-giving quality of *unconditional love*. Doctors

Duff and Campbell betray a tragic misunderstanding of the issue of love when they suggest that what they call "very defective individuals" possess "little or no hope of achieving 'meaningful humanhood.' For example, they have little or no capacity to love or be loved."[17] They actually believe a handicapped child cannot love and cannot *be loved!* Such an erroneous view of love seems inconceivable, yet I have to confess that my own understanding of unconditional love would be very limited if not for an experience I had a few years ago with some very special children.

Shortly after our marriage, my wife, Shirley, and I became involved in the lives of some of the more than one hundred retarded and physically handicapped children who were living in one Minneapolis home for the handicapped. We got to know many of these special children very well. In fact, as we worked with them for a time, it occurred to Shirley and me that God might be preparing us for such a special child in our own home. (As it turned out, this experience actually helped prepare us for an entire year of giving around-the-clock care to our critically ill daughter, Rachael, during the first difficult year of her life.)

When we began, we thought we were going to help and teach these handicapped children. Instead, they became *our* teachers. You may wonder how these children, whom many in our society deem to have no meaningful quality of life, could teach normal people anything. You might be thinking, "These unwanted kids must be very hard to love." But no, these children weren't hard to love. In fact, they modeled Christlike unconditional love to us. They immediately accepted us and pulled us into their lives. Unlike so many normal people in the world and in the Church, these children didn't care if we were needy or successful, rich or poor, black, brown, or white. They just smiled at us and hugged us and were grateful we were there. Their unconditional love taught me more about the free flowing love of God than any other experience in my life, and I am more of a human being and more like Christ today because of my experience with those mentally retarded and handicapped children.

Yet today, many children like those special children who loved me and taught me so much are today being aborted in the womb or starved in hospital incubators. They are being denied the chance to live because the sanctity of their lives has been subordinated to the question of the so-called quality of their lives.

I don't meant to suggest that caring for a handicapped child is an easy matter. A special child requires special effort and patience from his parents and from others in order to learn to walk, to talk, and to take care of himself. In rare cases, the handicapped child may even be uncontrollable, destructive, or unable to take care of his basic bodily needs. A child with a disability puts added strains on marital and family relationships. As Melinda Delahoyde has written:

> [Sometimes] the price we pay for life is very high. . . . [But] do we agree with so many around us who say that death is the best choice? No. We must firmly reject the idea that killing is compassionate. . . . The fact is that the child was born and that child reflects the image of God in some unique way. That image may be completely hidden from view. There may be tremendous emotional and physical problems to be solved for the family. But that is exactly the course we should take—devoting our time, energy and money to helping everyone live the best possible life in that situation. . . .
>
> [Christians] cannot lightly say to parents or society "choose life." In some situations, making that choice will bring years of sacrifice and pain. We must be there to ease that pain and share the burden with them.[18]

When a child is conceived with Down's Syndrome, spina bifida (cleft spine), cystic fibrosis, or some other handicap, parents today are presented with the choice to either love the child or dispose of him. It's a choice of life versus death, unconditional love versus dehumanization. As the parents of the disabled child choose life and love, fellow Christians have the opportunity to share the parent's burden and minister to "the least of these."

Similarly, doctors have a choice to either kill a defective unborn or newborn infant and dispose of the problem or to try to correct the defects, preserve the child's life, and give the parents hope for the future. In the course of preserving the sanctity of life, doctors often gain new knowledge and new techniques that can genuinely improve the quality of life for thousands of other children. No doctor ever gained valuable knowledge by aborting or starving a child to death.

John Powell relates an exchange that took place on a television talk show between the host and Dr. Victor Rosenblum, a pro-life professor of law and political science at Northwestern University. At one point, the questioner, unaware that Rosenblum was himself the father of a retarded child, asked him if he would approve of abortion if it were established that the fetus would be born mentally or physically defective. Rosenblum replied:

> Do you believe in love? . . . Do you really believe we are here to love one another? If you do, then you don't say, "I will love *you* because you have your mental faculties, and *you* because you are healthy, but *not you* because you have only one arm." True love does not discriminate in this way.
>
> If we really believe in love, and find a baby that will be born having no arms, we will say, "Baby, we are going to love you. We will make arms for you. We have many new skills now for doing this. And, Baby, if these arms don't work, we will *be* your arms. We will take care of you. You can be sure of that. You are one of us, a member of our human family, and we will always love you."[19]

Abortion is a sign that America no longer wants to love, is no longer willing to care. The legalization of abortion was the Supreme Court's response to a vocal minority's demand to be released from the duty to love. But our tolerance of abortion is a frightening indicator of how quickly we become dulled and receptive to the unthinkable and the unconscionable. The law is a powerful teacher, and legalized abortion has taught many Americans that human life has no intrinsic value—only the value others arbitrarily choose to place on it.

We now see that abortion does far more than destroy unborn life. Abortion destroys parental self-esteem and regard for life; it induces guilt and compounds violence. Abortion threatens the lives of those most in need of protection—the weak, the disabled, the abused, the neglected. Most of all, abortion destroys love.

Source Notes

1. Quoted in *Journal of Christian Nursing* (Summer 1985), p. 8.

2. Ibid., pp. 7,8.

3. Melinda Delahoyde, *Fighting for Life* (Ann Arbor: Servant Books, 1984), p. 10.

4. William A. Nolan, *The Baby in the Bottle* (New York: Coward, McCann & Geoghegan, Inc., 1978) pp. 245 and 252.

5. Katrina Maxtone-Graham, *Pregnant by Mistake* (New York: Liveright, 1973), p. 108.

6. Ibid., p. 33.

7. Ibid., p. 292.

8. Ibid., pp. 84 and 86.

9. James T. Burtchaell, *Rachel Weeping* (New York: Harper & Row, 1982), p. 26.

10. *Time* (September 5, 1983), p. 21.

11. Philip G. Ney, "Is Elective Abortion a Cause of Child Abuse?" *Sexual Medicine Today* (June 1980), p. 31.

12. Philip G. Ney, "A Consideration of Abortion Survivors," *Child Psychiatry and Human Development* (Spring 1983), p. 172.

13. Bernard N. Nathanson with Richard N. Ostling, *Aborting America* (Garden City, N.Y.: Doubleday, 1979), p. 190.

14. Vincent J. Fontana, *Somewhere a Child Is Crying* (New York: New American Library, 1976), pp. 215–216.

15. Burtchaell, *Rachel Weeping*, p. 119.

16. Ibid., p. 218.

17. Ibid., p. 299.

18. Delahoyde, *Fighting for Life*, pp. 71, 72, 76.

19. John Powell, *Abortion: The Silent Holocaust* (Allen, Tex.: Argus Communications, 1981), p. 8.

Chapter Six

The Aborting of Man

Into the Dark

And much it grieved my heart to think
What Man has made of Man.
> William Wordsworth
> *Lines Written*
> *in Early Spring*

If a man loses reverence for any
part of life, he will lose his
reverence for all of life.
> Albert Schweitzer

In June 1981, the *New York Times* reported the story of a woman pregnant with twins, one normal, one with a congenital defect. The woman elected to abort the defective child but keep the normal child. So, in an extraordinary and unprecedented procedure, doctors inserted a hypodermic syringe through the mother's abdomen and into the heart of the defective fetus. They then withdrew the blood from the perforated heart, and the fetus died.

Just one month later, the same newspaper carried a very similar story, this time about a woman pregnant with twins, one of whom had a defect in its urinary tract. A hypodermic syringe was inserted through the mother's abdomen and into the bladder of the affected fetus. The doctors successfully drained the perforated bladder of urine, and the life of this baby was saved.

At first glance, it would seem that the all-important contrast between these two stories lies in the fact that in one, a baby was killed and in the other, a baby was saved. Significantly, each story termed the operation "successful." But as we look more closely at how the *New York Times* wrote these two stories, we see that in the abortion story, the unborn twin who was killed was referred to exclusively as a "fetus." In the second story, the unborn life that was saved was called "an unborn child," a "baby," and a "girl."

Why are these two cases treated so differently by the very same newspaper? Why is one referred to with clinical detachment as a "fetus" while the other is accorded full human status with such terms as "child," "baby," and "girl"? Where is the dividing line between these two unborn children? They are distinguished from each other by only one factor: One is a wanted baby, the other is not. It would seem a wanted baby is a human being; an unwanted fetus is an inconvenient *thing* to be destroyed.

Abortion is not just the termination of a pregnancy, not just the elimination of an unwanted fetus. Abortion is simply infanticide *in utero*. It should not seem strange, then, that many advocates of abortion are also advocating the elimination of defective newborns within hours or days of their emergence from the womb. It requires a conscious effort of mental denial to evade the plain truth within each of us: In or out of the womb, a baby is a baby. The moment of birth is not a morally, emotionally, or intellectually satisfying boundary line. If a child should be legally protected after birth, he should be equally protected before birth. But if a child can be legally killed within the womb, why not outside of the womb, where possible defects can be more easily identified?

In retrospect, it seems clear that from the legalization of

abortion in 1973 to the killing of self-sustaining but unwanted babies today is only a small step. This is why Malcolm Muggeridge has called the legitimization of abortion
"a slippery slope," a term suggesting that once you take that
first downhill step, once you have accepted the first deadly
premise, there is nothing to stop you from sliding inexorably toward deeper and more frightening depths.

This is not to suggest that the only reason for opposing
abortion is to prevent some more terrifying evil down the
road. Abortion is truly a monstrous evil in its own right.
Unborn human life is no less human, no less alive, simply
because it has not yet made the transition beyond the
boundary of maternal flesh. If we are seeking grounds on
which to indict abortion as a morally abhorrent evil, we
need not look down the slippery slope toward distant,
dimly foreseen evils. The evil of abortion is abortion itself.

Yet we must not be blind to the direction in which abortion is inexorably drawing us.

The Slide Toward Infanticide

Whether the fetus is or is not a
human being is a matter of definition,
not fact; and we can define any way
we wish.

Garrett Hardin

Eventually, when public opinion is
prepared for it, no child should be
admitted into the society of the living
who would be certain to suffer any
social handicap. . . . This would imply
not only eugenic sterilization but
also euthanasia due to accidents of
birth which cannot be foreseen.

Millard S. Everett
Ideals of Life

The evidence that society is sliding toward acceptance of infanticide began to accumulate soon after *Roe vs. Wade* in 1973. Medical journals and news magazines began to carry editorials advocating a shift away from belief in the sanctity of life. Typical was this chillingly self-contradictory editorial statement in the *New Republic* (July 2, 1977):

> Those who believe a woman should be free to have an abortion must face the consequences of their beliefs. Metaphysical arguments about the beginning of life are fruitless. But there clearly is no logical or moral distinction between a fetus and a young baby; free availability of abortion cannot be reasonably distinguished from euthanasia. Nevertheless we are for it.[1]

This is cold and callous doublethink. The author of this editorial admits there is no logical or moral distinction between killing an unborn fetus (abortion) and killing unwanted infants or unwanted elderly people (euthanasia)—then concludes, *"nevertheless we are for it"*! Reason should dictate that if killing unborn human beings is indistinguishable from killing infants and old people, then the next logical step is to declare abortion wrong and seek to outlaw it. And yet, as any skier will tell you, it's a great deal easier to *schuss* the slopes than to trudge back up again, and many leaders of American opinion seem curiously eager to propel us all the faster down this perilous, slippery slalom. A few examples:

- The September 1970 issue of *California Medicine* carried a commentary advocating a "new medical ethic" based on "quality of life" over "sanctity of life." Significantly, the author of the piece proposed that this new ethic be promoted in an aggressively unethical way—with deceit, propaganda, and a casual disregard for the value of human life. An excerpt:

  The process of eroding the old ethic and substituting the new has already begun. It may be seen most clearly in changing attitudes toward human abortion. . . . Since the old ethic has not yet been fully displaced it has been necessary to separate the idea of abortion from the idea of killing, which continues to be socially abhorrent. The result has been a curious avoidance of the scientific fact, which everyone really knows, that human life begins at conception and is continuous whether intra- or extra-uterine until death. . . . It is suggested [that] this schizophrenic subterfuge is necessary because while a new ethic is being accepted the old one has not yet been rejected.[2]

- In a 1972 address to the American Association for the Advancement of Science, Yale University geneticist Y. Edward Hsia advocated mandatory prenatal tests so that defective unborn babies could be detected—and *compulsorily aborted.*

- Commenting on the Supreme Court decision in *Roe vs. Wade,* ethicist Joseph Fletcher (the leading proponent of "situation ethics") told *Time* magazine that the decision was part of "a welcome trend away from the sanctity-of-life attitude toward a quality-of-life ethic."[3] Later, in an article in *American Journal of Nursing,* he wrote that it was unreasonable to permit the abortion of "subhuman" (physically or mentally defective) fetuses while refusing to permit the euthanasia (deliberate killing) of "subhuman" people.[4] Fletcher sometimes refers to infanticide as "postnatal abortion."

- Some particularly startling proposals regarding the killing of newborn infants have come from Dr. James Watson and Dr. Francis Crick, who shared the 1962 Nobel Prize in physiology/medicine for their discovery of the famed double helix molecular structure of DNA. One would think that those few enlightened individuals who have peered into the deepest mysteries of biological life and pried open its secrets would have a special respect for human life. And yet it was Watson who stated in a 1973 interview, "If a child were not declared alive until three days after birth, then all parents could be allowed the choice only a few are given under the present system. The doctor could allow the child to die if the parents so chose, and save a lot of misery and suffering."[5] And Crick, in January 1978, told the Pacific News Service, "No newborn infant should be declared human until it has passed certain tests regarding its genetic endowment and . . . if it fails these tests it forfeits the right to live."

- In a 1976 article, Dr. Richard E. Harbin promoted the "new ethic" of death for defective infants. The physician, he wrote, should not base treatment on an outmoded sanctity of life idea, but should take into consideration the infant's quality of life and the costs—both emotional and financial—to the parents and society. He continues:

    As medical technology has advanced, so must medical ethics. The traditional ethics based on the sanctity of life must now give way to a code of ethics of the quality of life. . . . It is our duty to see that the development of medical ethics keeps in step with scientific developments.[6]

- In 1981, twenty-two legal, medical, and scientific experts testified before the Senate Subcommittee on Separation of Powers at a hearing on abortion. In the course of evaluating the merits of the Human Life Bill, the subcommittee was inquiring into the validity of the Supreme Court's reasoning in Roe vs. Wade. The witnesses were evenly divided between pro-abortion and pro-life positions, and it was clear to the subcommittee that the real issue was not "when does human life begin?" but "how much do we value human life?" The subcommittee concluded in part:

    Those witnesses who testified that science cannot say whether unborn children are human beings were speaking in every instance to the value question rather than the scientific question. . . . No witness challenged the scientific consensus that unborn children are "human beings" insofar as the term is used to mean living beings of the human species. Instead these witnesses invoked their value preferences to redefine the term "human being." . . .

A careful examination reveals the true nature of this line of argument. By redefining "human being" according to one's value preferences, one never has to admit believing that some human lives are unworthy of protection. Conveniently one can bury the value judgment that some human lives are not worth protecting beneath the statement that they are not human beings at all.[7]

- In 1983, the leading journal of pediatric medicine in America published a commentary on newborn life and medical ethics which included the following statement:

    If we compare a severely defective human infant with a dog or a pig . . . we will often find the nonhuman to have superior capacities . . . Only the fact that the defective infant is a member of the species *Homo sapiens* leads it to be treated differently from the dog or pig. But species membership alone is not relevant. . . . If we can put aside the obsolete and erroneous notion of the sanctity of all human life, we may start to look at . . . the quality of life that each human being has or can attain.[8]

Such statements by respected people of influence in our society should frighten us and compel us to take meaningful action. But understand this: These statements do not describe some nightmare of the far distant future. No, the Orwellian horrors of infanticide and euthanasia are with us *today*. The slippery slope is rapidly becoming an avalanche.

The Infant as Laboratory Rat

We are already witnessing the erosion
of our idea of man as something splendid
or divine, as a creature with freedom
and dignity. And clearly, if we come

to see ourselves as meat, then meat
we shall become.
                    Dr. Leon R. Kass
                    University of Chicago

[*Note*: The following section of this chapter contains
graphic and potentially disturbing material. While it is important that these facts be published, the reader should be
forewarned.]

Few people realized it at the time, but the *Roe vs. Wade*
decision made the killing of newborns almost inevitable.
Certainly there is no logical reason not to conduct "postnatal abortions" when the Supreme Court has already sanctioned the killing of infants in the womb—some of whom
are larger and older than many surviving premature infants.
In 1973, the Supreme Court declared open season on the
innocent, and today the innocent newborn are being starved
to death, drugged to death, smothered and strangled to
death in large numbers and with the complicity of parents
and physicians and our courts of law.

In June 1977, a prominent obstetrician was indicted for
allegedly strangling to death an infant who survived an attempted saline abortion at Westminster County Hospital in
California. At the trial, a colleague testified that this obstetrician twice attempted to strangle the saline-scalded baby
by throttling her with his hand, all the while complaining
about the lawsuits that would likely result from this
botched abortion. When it seemed clear that the baby was
not going to die easily, said the witness, the obstetrician
pondered aloud such options as injecting the child with po-
tassium chloride or drowning her in a pan of water. The
baby finally died, and the doctor was brought to trial for
strangling the infant. The trial ended in a hung jury after the
judge confused matters by interjecting a set of largely irrele-

vant instructions to the jury concerning the legal definition of death in California.

The Westminster County Hospital case points up how blurry and arbitrary the distinction is between abortion and the killing of newborns. Unsuccessful abortion procedures are virtually an everyday occurrence. One abortion authority has dubbed such failed abortions "the dreaded complication," since there is nothing so troubling to the death-dealing abortionist as the production of *life*. Understandably, precise figures on failed abortions are hard to obtain, since most are quietly covered up. But the Center for Disease Control in Atlanta has estimated that at least 400 to 500 abortions annually produce live infants, most of whom subsequently die or are killed.

One physician described the procedure for dealing with "the dreaded complication" to reporters for the *Philadelphia Inquirer*: "You want to know how they kill [the live-born infant]? They put a towel over his face so he can't breathe. And by the time they get him to the lab, he is dead."[9]

One grisly by-product of abortion and infanticide is experimentation involving freshly killed and even living aborted infants. Some examples:

- An affidavit filed by the state attorney general of Connecticut in a case before the U.S. Supreme Court (*Markle vs. Abele*, March 14, 1973) describes a case of human vivisection at Yale-New Haven Medical Center. According to the affidavit, a live-born male infant, born in the course of a hysterotomy abortion, was dissected while still alive and without anesthesia. The baby was observed to be breathing, moving, and urinating just moments before it was removed from the operating room and sent to a laboratory where its abdomen was said to have been opened and an organ or organs removed for study.

- In 1973, the federally funded U.S. National Institute of Health participated in a study in Finland in which a dozen "fresh" late-term fetuses were decapitated and their brains infused with chemicals so that their metabolic processes could be observed. When the results were reported to a meeting of the American Pediatric Society, *Medical World News* (June 8, 1973) reported that "no one even raised an eyebrow."

- The *New York Times Magazine* (October 19, 1975) reported on research in which living aborted infants were attached to artificial placentas and kept alive for several hours of "irregular gasping" while the heartbeat "slowed ... and eventually stopped." This research was awarded the Foundation Prize from the American Association of Obstetricians and Gynecologists.

- In several European countries, including France and Italy, the abortion industry has begun to supply aborted fetuses and fetal parts (preserved by freezing immediately after killing, or even while the fetus is still alive and moving) to laboratories for use in medical research and basic biological research. The European abortion industry is profitably exploiting a popular myth among European women that body cells from aborted human fetuses have rejuvenating properties, and include by-products of aborted fetuses in various cosmetics and skin creams.

  In the United States, many shampoos and cosmetics contain an ingredient called collagen, a protein-rich gelatinous material found in animal bones and cartilage. Unless the ingredient list of a product specifically states that it contains "animal collagen" or "bovine collagen," a "collagen-enriched" product may contain by-products of human abortion.

- In the United States, a new rabies vaccine approved by the Food and Drug Administration in 1980 is derived from the lung tissue of aborted fetuses. Meanwhile, at the University of Colorado Medical Center in Denver, fetal organs are often grafted into the bodies of mice so that new drugs can be tested on them.

- Researchers in the United States are planning to introduce a treatment for a particular type of diabetes, using insulin-producing cells (islets) from the endocrine pancreas of aborted fetuses. This treatment, which was developed at the Australian National University in 1983, requires that the pancreas be removed quickly from "fresh" fetuses, so that the islets can be isolated and cultured for transplant into diabetic patients.

It is truly ironic that at the same time some doctors and scientists are using unborn human beings for horrible experiments, other doctors are employing their healing skills to save the unborn. Ultrasound imaging techniques now enable doctors to detect and surgically treat such once fatal problems as blockages in the urinary tract and accumulation of cerebrospinal fluid in the brain (hydrocephalus). Techniques are even being developed that will soon enable an unborn child with a heart or diaphragm problem to be temporarily born—removed from the womb, surgically treated, and returned to the womb so that the infant can continue to grow and become healed in the safest, most nurturing environment possible.

In the same hospital or medical center, one unborn human infant may be treated as a human life to be heroically saved while another of roughly the same gestational age may be treated as little more than a laboratory rat. Clearly, the distinction is one of purely arbitrary values. When the Supreme Court allowed unborn infants to be killed without cause in 1973, the unborn became nonpersons, without rights, without protection.

Cost/Benefit Analysis

Oh God! that bread should be so dear,
And flesh and blood so cheap!

Thomas Hood

The rich get richer, and inherit the meek.

Mark Heard

The image of God that once gave us our ennobled view of man is fast becoming a lost image, effaced and ultimately replaced by mechanistic and animalistic images of man. Abortion is both symptom and factor in the rapid devaluation of our species from *Man* (with a capital M) to mere meat, priced to sell at a few dollars per pound.

Today, cost/benefit analyses are used to decide who lives and who dies. One past president of the National Abortion Rights Action League put it this way: "A legal abortion for a woman on welfare now costs the state $150, but if the abortion were not performed the state would pay out $60,000 over an 18-year span to support the mother and child on welfare."[10] The same bottom-line logic is being applied to the handicapped, and the conclusion that is being reached with increasing frequency is that it is simply *cheaper* to abort the defective unborn, starve the handicapped newborn, and let our seriously ill and elderly perish of neglect. To love and to care, you see, is costly.

It all comes down to the fact that there are two ways to view human beings. There is the biblical view—God's own cost/benefit analysis of man—which sees human beings as possessing exquisite value. Because we are made in God's own likeness, human life is precious—so precious that God would give His Son Jesus Christ to be cruelly put to death in order to redeem fallen human beings and restore His image to them.

Opposing the biblical view is the secular view, which sees man as a highly evolved animal, without intrinsic or absolute value. According to this view we can, if we wish, genetically refashion and revise man, weed out defective individuals, breed for bodily perfection and the greatest economy to society. This view of man was really inevitable in a post-Christian age, an age of moral and ethical anarchy, unmoored from the foundation of Judeo-Christian values. As Francis Bacon observed almost 400 years ago, "Our humanity would be a poor thing but for the Divinity that stirs within us." That divinity has been lost by modern man, and when the image of divinity is lost, then man as *Man* becomes lost, too.

Once we begin to see ourselves as animals, then what I would call a veterinary view of human life becomes inevitable. The quality of life ethic (which has largely replaced the sanctity of life ethic) is rooted in this veterinary view of human life. As everyone is aware, there is a reasonable limit to the value we place on animal life. We use some animals for food, some as beasts of burden, and some as companions or pets. Whenever we find it necessary to kill an animal, we do so as quickly and painlessly as possible. When a dog or cat or horse suffers incurably or cannot be economically treated, we put the poor creature out of its misery. This is not only sensible and humane, but it's required by laws that impose strong penalties on those who treat animals with cruelty or neglect.

But now the same ethic is being applied to human beings under the term *mercy killing*. Those with a veterinary view of human life now ask, "If man is just a highly evolved animal, then why not do the same to suffering people? Why not simply put people to sleep when they have become too much of a burden?" Under a sanctity of life ethic, such a question is unthinkable; under a quality of life ethic, such a question is inevitable.

Yet there is something in most people that prevents this veterinary ethic from being carried to its logical conclusion. Perhaps it's a pang of conscience, or maybe it's simple fear of criminal prosecution, but suffering people are hardly ever simply put to sleep like animals. When the decision to kill is combined with this vestigial trace of human conscience, so that the hand of the mercy killer is stayed from acting directly and swiftly, the result is amazingly cruel and inhumane. Today, our society executes murderers by swift and painless lethal injection, while starving its innocents over days and weeks of agony.

The SPCA would never consider starving a dog or cat as an act of mercy. Yet for quality of life physicians, cruel starvation is the method of choice. Baby Doe, for example, took six days to die of starvation. Compared to many infanticide cases, Baby Doe's six-day ordeal of dying was relatively brief. Most newborn infanticide victims take a week or more to die after food and water have been withdrawn (longer than it would most adults), because they are born with a greater proportion of stored fat and water in their tissues.

But it's not only babies who are starved to death for the sake of quality of life. In Los Angeles in 1983, a man named Clarence L. Herbert, who was comatose following a heart attack and surgery, was removed from a respirator. When he continued to breathe on his own, the man's family and doctor decided to withdraw all intravenous nourishment and water, and Herbert died six days later. That same year, a New Jersey court ordered that an eighty-four-year-old woman (who was aware but mentally incompetent and completely dependent on intravenous feedings), could be starved to death. This decision was later reversed by an appellate court, and the woman was spared.

The Revulsion Threshold

At Nuremburg the prosecution argued
that the killing programs unfolded
one from another, that the genocide
of the six millionth Jew was somehow
unleashed by the morphine overdose
of the first [handicapped] child.

James Burtchaell
Rachel Weeping

The quality of life proponents have presented us with a monstrous contradiction: starvation to end suffering. They have turned some of our hospitals, ostensibly places of care and healing, into places where hideous atrocities are committed, where suffering and death are deliberately inflicted in the perverse and incomprehensible rationale that quality of life is being preserved.

We are beginning to realize that the quality of life ethic is destroying the very quality of life it is intended to uphold. This new ethic joins the mutually exclusive terms *mercy* and *killing* into a single self-contradictory phrase, then inflicts this "mercy" by horrible means of starvation. To accept the quality of life ethic is to live in a state of contradiction and to talk in incoherent terms. It is becoming increasingly clear that we can never preserve the quality of human life until we affirm its sanctity. All human life eventually loses value, meaning, and quality unless we affirm that every life is worth living.

Tragically, our cultural attitude toward life is on a sliding scale—a scale that is tilted steeply downhill. Values and beliefs that used to hold stable for hundreds or thousands of years in older cultures can crumble in less than a decade in today's fast-paced information age. What was unthinkable a few short years ago is commonplace today. Attitudes toward life and death and human suffering are fluid, determined not according to reason or principle but convenience and utility. Abhorrent practices soon become accepted practices.

Under the quality of life ethic, all that prevents us from descending to the next rung of dehumanizing treatment of human beings is what I would call *the revulsion threshold.* People can only stomach so much horror at any one time. Horror must be measured out slowly, bit by bit, in order to become widely accepted. Thus, we gradually become acclimated today to what revolted and sickened us yesterday. Our revulsion threshold—our level of tolerance for the intolerable—is a moving point on a continuous downward-tending line.

In 1965, unborn babies were still viewed as unborn babies, not "products of conception." The comparatively high revulsion threshold of the majority of Americans prevented society from sanctioning the casual slaughter of unborn infants on demand. Pro-abortion referenda were soundly voted down in every state where they were proposed. Planned Parenthood preached contraception, not abortion, and its literature stated, "Abortion kills the life of a baby once it has begun." American society generally deemed all children, including the handicapped, to be precious human beings worthy of love and care; infanticide against the newborn was totally unthinkable.

In 1975, two years after *Roe vs. Wade*, 852,000 babies were being aborted. Planned Parenthood had turned aggressively pro-abortion, having performed some 35,000 abortions in its own abortoriums, while referring untold numbers of women to other facilities for abortions. Moreover, Planned Parenthood embarked on an aggressive five-year plan for its own abortion facilities, with a goal of 80,000 abortions a year by 1980. Meanwhile, newborn infanticide had quietly begun in scattered hospitals around the country. The revulsion threshold was slipping badly.

By 1985, more than 1.5 million unborn infants were being sacrificed to abortion every year. Infanticide against the newborn was now a medical commonplace—still handled quietly, but without notable protest. Scattered incidents of euthanasia against the elderly began to make the headlines. The revulsion threshold continued to plummet.

What can we look forward to by 1995 and beyond? Malcolm Muggeridge suggested a disturbing answer in his 1975 essay, "What the Abortion Argument Is About":

> Our western way of life has come to a parting of the ways. . . . Either we go on with the process of shaping

our own destiny without reference to any higher being than man, deciding ourselves how many children should be born, when and what varieties, which lives are worth continuing and which should be put out, from whom spare parts—kidneys, hearts, genitals, brain boxes even—shall be taken and to whom allotted.

Or we can draw back, seeking to understand and fall in with our Creator's purpose for us rather than to pursue our own; in true humility praying, as the founder of our religion and civilization taught us, Thy will be done.

This is what the abortion controversy is all about and what the euthanasia controversy will be about when, as must inevitably happen soon, it arises. The logical sequel to the destruction of what are called "unwanted children" will be the elimination of what are called "unwanted lives"—a legislative measure which so far in all human history only the Nazi government has ventured to enact.

In this sense, the abortion controversy is the most vital and relevant of all. . . . If we transgress against the very basis of our mortal existence, becoming our own gods and our own universe, then we shall surely and deservedly perish from the earth.[11]

Those who would engineer the human species have begun by eliminating certain categories of unwanteds, beginning with Down's Syndrome unborn and newborn. They have proceeded next to the medically dependent elderly. What will be the next category of people whose life is "not worthy to be lived"? The blind? The deaf? Retarded adults? Alzheimer's disease cases? People in wheelchairs? People with cystic fibrosis? Diabetes? AIDS? Cancer? Neurological problems? Psychiatric problems? The genetically impure? Criminals? Derelicts and the chronically unemployed? Undocumented aliens? Everyone over eighty?

Unthinkable, you say? Yes, it's all completely unthinkable—today.

Tomorrow, however, the revulsion threshold will surely have moved still further, unless we find a way to replace the downwardly mobile revulsion threshold with a stable moral currency. The line between life and death can be logically, scientifically drawn at one place and only one place: the point of conception. Any other point is purely arbitrary, and thus subject to change. Under the new ethic, more and more kinds of people will inevitably be seen as unwanted, and they will be weeded out. The image of God will be aborted, replaced by a new image—the image of what man has made of *Man*.

In *The Screwtape Letters*, C. S. Lewis's demonic correspondent Screwtape observes, "The safest road to Hell is the gradual one—the gentle slope, soft underfoot, without sudden turnings, without milestones, without signposts."[12] That is the slope we are treading today. Abortion is rapidly accelerating the hellward side of humanity—down, down, down the slope of dehumanization and alienation to the abortion of man as *Man*. Our path is a gentle one, with no sudden turnings, no milestones, no signposts. It leads us irresistibly toward a brave new world: a gleaming, alluring, sanitized hell of physical perfection, genetic and racial purity, and moral extinction.

Source Notes

1. William A. Nolen, *The Baby in the Bottle* (New York: Coward, McCann & Geoghegan, Inc., 1978), p. 230.

2. *California Medicine* (Vol. 113, No. 3, September 1970), pp. 67, 68.

3. *Time* (January 29, 1973), p. 47.

4. *American Journal of Nursing* (73:679, 1973).

5. *Time* (May 28, 1973), p. 104.

6. *Pediatric Nursing* (July/August 1976), quoted in *Abortion: The Silent Holocaust* by John Powell, p. 133.

7. "Report to the Committee on the Judiciary Regarding the Human Life Bill—S. 158," 97th Congress, First Session, pp. 11, 12.

8. "Sanctity of Life, Quality of Life," *Pediatrics* (Vol. 72, No. 1, 1983), p. 18.

9. *The Philadelphia Inquirer* (August 2, 1981), p. 17.

10. John Powell, *Abortion: The Silent Holocaust* (Allen, Tex.: Argus Communications, 1981), p. 102.

11. Malcolm Muggeridge, "What the Abortion Argument Is About," *Human Life Review* (Vol. 1, No. 3, 1975).

12. C. S. Lewis, *The Screwtape Letters* (New York: Macmillan Co., 1943), p. 65.

Chapter Seven

The Compassionate War

The Great Escape

Don't *say* things. What you *are*
stands over you the while, and
thunders so that I cannot hear
what you say to the contrary.
Ralph Waldo Emerson
Social Aims

Tom and I were close friends. We grew up together in a
small town in Iowa and were roommates at Tarkio College
in Missouri. After graduation, I went on to seminary and
Tom went with Church World Service to feed and care for
hungry children in India. That was about fifteen years ago.

Not long ago, Tom and I were together again for the first
time in a long while. As we were chatting and getting reac-
quainted, he told me some of his experiences in India and I
shared with him a bit of my life as an evangelical pastor in
America. As we were talking openly together, he said one
thing that really stuck in my mind: "You know, Ron, the

149

thing you evangelicals need to learn is that words are cheap."

Tom was absolutely right. The credibility of the Church of Jesus Christ—and particularly that part of the Church that calls itself evangelical—lies right here: Do we really believe that our witness for Christ is more than buttons we wear on our lapels or bumper stickers we paste on our cars? Words are cheap. Evangelical action speaks much louder than evangelical words.

The book you hold in your hands is one of many books you can read about the pro-life issue. Just about anybody can write a book. But there is one thing about *this* book that's certain: Either it's just one more book about an issue or it's the testimony of someone who is seeking to live obediently after the pattern of Jesus Christ, caring for the least and the last and the lost. God alone will judge my life, my work, and my words. The point is that the 80,000 or so words in this book are cheap words if they're not backed up by costly, obedient action in my own life. The same is true for you and every other person who claims to be pro-life.

A lot of people have opinions, and they'll gladly give them to you. They'll tell you what's wrong with the world, with the country, and with the Church. In fact, most people have an opinion on abortion. The problem is that no one ever changed the world with opinions.

There's a world of difference between opinions and *convictions*. An opinion is just an attitude, a notion, a point of view. A person with an opinion doesn't have to act; he can simply talk. But a conviction is a deeply rooted belief that won't let go of you, won't let you rest, won't let you be content until you have taken action on your beliefs and have begun to make a difference in the world. A person of Christian convictions is a person whose heart is broken over the things that break the heart of God. Everyone in the world has opinions, but people of conviction are rare in this world.

Let me make a broad generalization: *The average Christian*

today is not concerned with involvement; he is concerned with escape.
Just take a look around the evangelical landscape, at all the
books, marketing gimmicks, and Christian television and
radio programs devoted to "Christianized" self-fulfillment
and self-indulgence, the "possibility thinking" gospel, the
"success" gospel, and pop-eschatology (what you might call
"late-great-escapism"). The average Christian no longer
seeks to take risks for God; he wants worldly security. He
doesn't want to serve God; he wants God to serve him.

Many of us in the Church today expect God to give us
fulfillment, material success, health, and prosperity. Not
only that, but some of us feel we are entitled to all these
things—that God has promised it to us, and that God has no
greater purpose in the world than to look after our wants
and wishes. And if things should happen to get really bad in
the world, well, times of tribulation were prophesied in the
Bible, anyway, and it just means Jesus is going to return
soon and take us out of this miserable world.

In his book *The Mustard Seed Conspiracy*, Dr. Tom Sine,
director of the Christian relief and development agency
World Concern, calls this heretical mind-set "the Great Escape." He tells of one encounter with a college coed on a
Christian campus in the northwest during a lecture he was
giving on the future of the world and Christian activism.
This young woman stood and asked, "Do you realize if we
start feeding hungry people things won't get worse, and if
things don't get worse, Jesus won't come?" From her expression and tone of voice, Sine knew she was completely
serious. He adds:

> Unfortunately, I have discovered the coed's question
> doesn't reflect an isolated viewpoint. Rather, it betrays a
> wide-spread misunderstanding of biblical eschatology
> (having to do with the last days) that seems to permeate
> much of contemporary Christian consciousness. I be-
> lieve this misunderstanding of God's intentions for the
> human future is seriously undermining the effectiveness

of the people of God in carrying out His mission in a world of need. . . . When we look into the future all we see is the world going "to hell in a handbasket." . . . There is the feeling that, while such suffering is undeniably tragic, God intended it to happen and there is no point in our working to try to alleviate it.[1]

From *The Mustard Seed Conspiracy* by Tom Sine, copyright © 1981; used by permission of Word Books, Publisher, Waco, Texas.

The heresy of the Great Escape takes many bizarre and extreme forms, such as that recently noted in the "Newsmakers" section of *Newsweek*:

Not long ago, the Rev. Terry Cole-Whittaker was preaching from her southern California pulpit that "you can have it all now" and that prosperity was a "divine right." But on a recent trip to India, Cole-Whittaker saw the light: she now realizes that "people can live in poverty and be happy," and will give her last sermon on Easter Sunday. Cole-Whittaker's revelation was well-timed: her enterprises took in over $6 million last year, but managed to wind up $400,000 in debt. A spokesman insists the church's financial problems had nothing to do with the reverend's decision. She herself says she's stepping down because "world saviors do not last on this planet"; her supporters say it's a case of "burnout." The next stop on Cole-Whittaker's spiritual path will probably be Hawaii, where she means to "sit on the beach and only get up to get a papaya."[2]

Now, perhaps you and I would never talk about the "happy" people who live in poverty. You and I would never jet off to a tropical paradise while the rest of the world slides into hell. You and I would never sit on the beach and eat papaya while the world around us dies of starvation and abortion and war and race hatred.

Or would we? More to the point, *do we?*

I submit that, to a frightening degree, that is precisely what we do. We in the American Church have largely bought into the lie of the Great Escape. God has called us to roll up our sleeves, to get involved, to get our hands dirty, and to get His work done—but like Jonah turning away from Nineveh, we have sought only escape. We escape into our material pursuits, into our religious pursuits, into our social pursuits, while our world sinks deeper and deeper in its pain and despair.

Advancing Against Hell

> What good is it, my brothers, if a man
> claims to have faith but has no deeds?
> Can such faith save him? Suppose a
> brother or sister is without clothes
> and daily food. If one of you says to
> him, "Go, I wish you well; keep warm
> and well fed," but does nothing about
> his physical needs, what good is it?
> In the same way, faith by itself, if it
> is not accompanied by action, is dead.
>   James 2:14–17

Many Christians in last century understood that the gospel of Jesus Christ is a call to *involvement* in the world's pain and sorrow. The gospel has not changed since an English politician named William Wilberforce (1759–1833) was converted to evangelical Christianity in 1784. Moved by the love of Christ, Wilberforce led the fight against slavery in the British Parliament—a fight that ended with the passage of the Slavery Abolition Act, one month after his death. The gospel has not changed since William Carey (1761–1834) exhorted, "Expect great things from God! Attempt great things for God!" and went on to India, preaching Christ, founding schools, promoting agricultural development, and fighting slavery and oppression. The gospel has not changed since Charles Finney (1792–1875), professor of theology at Oberlin College in Ohio, preached the gospel with evangelical zeal while on the front lines of the antislavery movement. The gospel has not changed since a wealthy Russian nobleman named Leo Tolstoy (1828–1910) encountered Christ, foreswore his title, freed his peasant servants, assigned all the rights to his books to benefit debtors and paupers, and joined the ranks of the hard-toiling poor.

People of Christian conviction have led every major social reform in American history: the drive to abolish slavery, the temperance movement, the peace movement, the feminist movement (before it was taken over by pro-abortion forces), and the fight against racial injustice, America's apartheid. All of these issues were on the biblical Christian agenda long before they became part of the secular social agenda. Because people of Christian conviction became involved and waded neck deep into the fight for justice, American society was deeply, directly, and lastingly changed.

Today, God calls you and me, men and women of authentic Christian conviction, to involvement in the suffering and injustice of our fallen world. He calls us to a life of serving, not being served. He calls us to obedience. He calls us to a life of risk taking and costly discipleship. He calls us to be consistently, authentically pro-life—pro human life and pro eternal life—in every aspect of our lives. We are freedom fighters in a rebellion against the forces that hold our world in chains of death and misery.

What, then is the Christian strategy for the pro-life revolution?

I believe our plan of attack is found in the life and teaching of Jesus Christ, for it is in His own words that we truly find the Christian manifesto as proclaimed by the founder of Christianity. Jesus was the most kind and compassionate man who ever lived, yet He preached the hardest and most confrontational gospel ever preached. If we ignore the hard demand of Christ upon our lives, then how can we honestly call ourselves Christians?

Someone once said that the hottest places in hell are reserved for those who, in a time of moral crisis, maintained their neutrality. Certainly, we live in a time of deep moral crisis today. I believe one of the great tragedies of the American Church in the 1980s is that it has maintained its neutrality. We in the Church have not been willing to apply the hard words of Jesus to ourselves and to the culture in which we live.

I suspect that many of us today don't really know why people wanted to nail Jesus Christ to a cross. Was it because He said, "Love one another"? I don't think so. I don't think anyone was ever crucified because he preached the message "love one another." Rather, I believe that what stirred up the people of Jesus' day to anger and murder was that Jesus told them what loving one another would *mean* in specific, practical terms. It was a confrontational message then, and it is just as confrontational today.

Many of us don't realize how alien the values of the Sermon on the Mount are to our own values. The words are familiar, perhaps, but the meaning of the words is hard for us to absorb. "Surely," we think, "Jesus didn't mean that *literally*." We put on our cultural blinders, and we dilute and spiritualize and minimize God's clear, unvarnished truth for our lives.

Jesus preached, "Blessed are the poor in spirit." We may try to harmonize that with the deeply rooted spirit of pride and self-sufficiency that typifies our American values, but we can't. Jesus said, "Love your enemies." We may try to harmonize that with the revenge ethic; the winning is everything ethic; an eye for an eye, a tooth for a tooth—but we can't. Jesus preached, "Pray for those who despitefully use you." We may try to harmonize that with looking out for number one and don't get mad, get even—but we can't.

Jesus has drawn a clear and impassable line between the Kingdom of God and the kingdom of this world, between Kingdom living and worldly living, between Christian values and the corrupt values of this dying age. He begins with the Beatitudes, a bold description of what Kingdom people are supposed to be. These are the kind of people who will make a revolutionary difference for life and for the Kingdom of God in a world of sin and death:

> Blessed are the poor in spirit,
>> for theirs is the kingdom of heaven.
> Blessed are those who mourn,
>> for they will be comforted.
> Blessed are the meek,
>> for they will inherit the earth.
> Blessed are those who hunger and thirst
>> for righteousness, for they will be filled.
> Blessed are the merciful,
>> for they will be shown mercy.
> Blessed are the pure in heart,
>> for they will see God.
> Blessed are the peacemakers,
>> for they will be called sons of God.
> Blessed are those who are persecuted
>> because of righteousness,
>> for theirs is the kingdom of heaven.
>> Matthew 5:3–10

Some Bible scholars have suggested that this word *blessed* means "happy"—though it's hard to understand how those who mourn and those who are persecuted should feel happy in their suffering. Others have suggested that *blessed* indicates some sort of reward or benefit that accrues to the account of those who are poor in spirit, and I believe there is some truth to that. But I'm convinced that the deepest truth that Jesus discloses to us in the Beatitudes is that God will pronounce His blessing, His approval, His affirmation upon those who demonstrate the Kingdom of God in their lives.

In Matthew 5:13–16, Jesus tells us that we, as His followers, are the salt of the earth and the light of the world. We preserve and illuminate the world. We are agents of revolution, engaged in a war, and there is no room for neutrality. We are either on the front lines, advancing against the gates of hell, or we are in retreat. There is nothing in between.

A Revolution of Love

Behold, I do not give lectures
or a little charity. When I give,
I give myself.
                                Walt Whitman

In the middle of the last century, there was a man who looked at the life of Christ and found there a plan for turning the world upside down. He saw that Jesus, a man in His early thirties, had invested three years of ministry into twelve ordinary human beings and had thereby transformed history.

In the life of Christ, this man found a four-point strategy for revolution: (1) the revolutionary must become aware of the people, their needs, their hurts, their plight; (2) the revolutionary must withdraw from the people for a time of study and reflection and meditation, during which time he must discern exactly what message he has to give to the people; (3) once the message has been formulated, the revolutionary must not deliver it to the masses, but entrust it to a small nucleus of dedicated people who are willing to accept and live out his hard teaching; and (4) the revolutionary must spend his life with that small nucleus of dedicated people and pour his life into them.

So this man proceeded to carry out the plan for revolution he had found in the life of Christ. For many long months, day after day, he descended into the musty seclusion of the basement of the British Museum Library in London. For long hours every day, he obsessively poured himself into his studies, discerning the historical framework for his revolution, formulating the message that would one day be published as *The Communist Manifesto*. Today, more than a billion human souls live under regimes that profess the revolutionary strategy of Karl Marx—a strategy he took from the life of Jesus Christ.

Marx's revolutionary successor, Nicolai Lenin, once noted the contrast between the dedication of the Communists to their cause versus the commitment most Christians seem to have toward the cause of Christ. "It is my greatest hope," wrote Lenin, "that those who call themselves Christians will never read their Bibles, for if they do they will find in its pages a revolution that makes ours appear weak, passive, and docile by comparison."

Lenin was right. The revolution of love proclaimed by Jesus Christ makes every other form of revolution, activism, and social reform appear impotent by comparison. Tragically, we in the Church have neglected to live out what we say we believe. In fact, we have failed to even discover what our revolution is really all about. To be agents of change in a dying world, we need to open the Word of God and discover His agenda for change.

Surveys show that 70 percent of Americans say they are church members, and 60 percent say their religious beliefs are very important to them. Yet a recent survey commissioned by *Christianity Today* revealed that of all Protestants who would term themselves "serious followers of Jesus Christ" only 18 percent ever study the Bible. The Bible has become the book that every Christian owns (usually in several translations), every Christian reveres, every Christian honors—but few Christians study.

Jesus Christ studied the Scriptures. Before beginning His public ministry at age thirty, he studied until He knew the Scriptures so well that He was able to quote freely from them when He preached to the people, when He confronted the Pharisees, and when He rebuked Satan's attack in the wilderness. The revolution begun by Jesus Christ changed the world; it is a revolution that is rooted in the Word of God.

Martin Luther studied the Scriptures, and there he found the basis and plan for the Protestant Reformation—indeed, the Protestant revolution. Luther founded a revolt against corrupt religious authority, and his revolution was rooted in the authority and the truth of Scripture.

The same is true of Paul the apostle, Saint Augustine, John Calvin, John Wycliffe, William Tyndale, John Wesley, Dietrich Bonhoeffer, C.S. Lewis, Henrietta Mears, Billy Graham, and every other person who has had a pivotal role in Christian history. The one factor they all have in common is that they gave themselves to an intensive, lifelong study of the Word of God.

The Church in America is numerically large but woefully ineffectual regarding the major issues of our time: abortion, hunger, peace, moral deterioration. Judging from our numbers alone, our society and our world should have been deeply penetrated and permeated by the gospel by this time, but they have not.

Why?

I believe this is largely due to the fact that we in the Church speak to the world not with one voice, but with many. There is confusion in the Church as to what our mission in the world really is. And I'm convinced that the reason for this confusion is that we have formulated our agenda for action from our culture and its values, rather than from the Bible. We have liberal Christians who advocate the liberal political agenda, conservative Christians who are pushing the conservative political agenda, and moderate Christians who walk gingerly down the middle of the political road. But there are comparatively few Christians who are seeking to promote an authentically Kingdom originated, biblically derived agenda in our time.

The Failure of Left and Right

> Both conservative and liberal religion
> have been much too eager to meet the
> world on its own terms. Despite their
> theological polarities . . . they have
> both tended to define the meaning
> of Christian faith according to the
> world views and lifestyles each has
> adopted from the secular culture.
> In each case, the *whole* deposit
> of revelation is neglected or
> selectively appropriated, and
> conformity is the inevitable result.
>
> Jim Wallis
> *Agenda for Biblical People*

The terms *liberal* and *conservative* used to be invested with a certain amount of meaningful content. A liberal was a person who believed in (and ostensibly practiced) liberality—that is, generosity and compassion. A liberal could be counted on to champion the poor, the oppressed, the disadvantaged, the exploited, the neglected. A conservative was a person who sought to conserve and protect the most important values and ideals of our heritage: morality, decency, honor, love of family, love of country, justice, and fair play. Neither liberalism nor conservatism can claim such nobility today.

Modern liberalism has been tried, and it has failed. Today's liberalism tends to be elitist and uninvolved. Liberals tend to have opinions rather than convictions. For example, they will talk about racial equality and advocate busing for racial integration while sending their own children to private schools. Liberals tend to see the government as being responsible for solving social problems and delivering human services. Liberalism has acquired the image of being the fashionable, intellectual, enlightened, and reasonable way of thinking.

Many liberals will even say something like, "I'm *personally* against abortion, but I don't want to impose my views on other people; every woman should be free to make her own choice." A person who confesses to pro-life leanings in a room full of liberals will likely find himself despised or pitied as a rigid fundamentalist. After all, what could be more reasonable than the idea that every woman should have total reproductive freedom?

If modern liberalism is the failed social experiment of the recent past, modern conservatism is the failing social experiment of the present. Today's conservatism tends to be resistant to change, pragmatic rather than idealistic, and self-centered rather than self-sacrificing. Conservatives support the free-market system because they genuinely believe that when all are free to pursue as much gain as they can for themselves, everybody benefits. Today's conservatives tend to be more concerned with conserving their own security and wealth than with intangibles such as values and principles. They tend to resent liberal "giveaway" programs for the needy, though they have no objection to spending a trillion dollars on warfare welfare for defense contractors (all in the name of national security). The problems of the poor, reasons the conservative, really have no solution, since the poor are essentially lazy. When many of today's conservatives call themselves pro-life, they really mean they are anti-abortion, period.

Does either of these descriptions sound like the Kingdom way of life that Jesus modeled for us? I'm convinced that one of the great sins of twentieth century Christianity is that we have allowed the secular doctrines of our culture to set the agenda for the Church. We have ignored the admonition of the apostle Paul: "Do not conform any longer to the pattern of this world, but be transformed by the renewing of your mind. Then you will be able to test and approve what God's will is—his good, pleasing and perfect will" (Romans 12:2).

Paul is telling us that God expects us to become Christian nonconformists in the midst of our American culture. "Do not conform!" he says in effect, "but rather, be transformed! Challenge the right of this present age to set the agenda for your life!" God's good and perfect agenda for social action can only be found as we shed our preconceptions, reject conformity with the world, and renew our minds in conformity with God's Word.

Mainline denominations have tended to uncritically espouse the secular liberal line, exemplified by the liberal church's usual position favoring abortion-on-demand. In the same way, fundamentalists and conservative evangelicals have heedlessly equated religious conservatism with political conservatism, and as a result the gospel has increasingly become linked with an attitude of neglect (if not contempt) for the poor; support of right-wing repression in such places as South Africa and Latin America; and the unchecked stockpiling of nuclear weapons.

God's plan for Christian activism does not conform to any secular agenda, whether from the left, right, or middle. Liberal, conservative, and moderate ideologies are all part of the passing things of this world. God's plan of action for our lives can only be found as we pull ourselves away from the dizzying maelstrom of highly charged rhetoric that characterizes our political climate and turn toward God in prayer and meditation in His Word.

I affirm the words of Henri Nouwen: "In a world that victimizes us by its compulsions, we are called to solitude where we can struggle against our anger and greed and let our new self be born in the loving encounter with Jesus Christ. It is in this solitude that we became compassionate people, deeply aware of the solidarity of our brokenness with all humanity and ready to reach out to anyone in need."[3]

In our solitude with God, we re-examine and rediscover the life of our example, Jesus Christ. We find that though He was the Son of God, He came as a servant. He lived a life of prayer, contemplation, simplicity, and selflessness. He identified with the poor, the oppressed, and the imprisoned, and He opposed injustice and the abuse of power. His mission in the world is ours as well. Caring for the poor, identifying with the oppressed, saving those who are threatened with death, ministering to those who are in prison—these are not liberal or conservative concerns. These are *Kingdom* concerns.

Citizens of the Kingdom

Our citizenship is in heaven. . . .
Philippians 3:20

Not long ago, my friend Ron Sider, national president of Evangelicals for Social Action, was speaking to a group of Christian leaders in Denver. At the conclusion of his talk on the subject of justice for the poor and disadvantaged, someone in the audience stood and hotly accused him of being a socialist. Ron didn't get angry. Instead, he listened politely, then replied simply, "I'm opposed to the injustice of centralized economics, whether in the form of a socialistic government or a capitalistic multinational corporation." That's a statement by a man who comes not from the right, not from the left, not from the middle of the road, but from the Kingdom.

More than any other concern now facing us, the pro-life issue urgently needs to be rescued from captivity to any secular political agenda. The right of the unborn to live is not a conservative concern. It is a Kingdom concern, a Christian concern. Today there are hopeful signs that liberals and conservatives are beginning to work together in their common concern for life.

In the Christian Action Council, compassionate Christians of various persuasions have discarded their political labels, put on true Christian compassion, and formed hundreds of crisis pregnancy centers across the country. These centers offer counseling and assistance to women so that babies can be born, not aborted.

For more than two decades, the cause of equal rights for women has been tragically linked with the unjust demand for "abortion rights." Today, however, there are growing numbers of feminists who have come out strongly in their opposition to abortion. Some feminist organizations now operate homes for women and infants, find foster homes for unwed mothers, and seek to influence legislation and educate the public to the fact that abortion is a crime with two victims: the unborn and their mothers. For example, Feminists for Life (which was founded by Pat Goltz after she was expelled from the National Organization for Women because of her outspoken pro-life stance) currently seeks to have both the Equal Rights Amendment (which would protect the rights of women) and the Human Life Amendment (which would protect unborn life) added to the United States Constitution. And Women Exploited by Abortion, a national self-help organization, offers counseling, emotional support, and spiritual guidance for women who have been traumatized by abortion.

Tom Sine describes the Kingdom agenda to which God calls us in His Word and in the example of Jesus Christ:

> All Christians need to be actively involved in influencing the directions of the government. We must be the voice of conscience speaking out on ethical issues like the family, abortion, and social values, and challenging the abuse of power by those who control resources. Certainly the church must take a leading role in rapidly activating and expanding informal, low-cost care networks to supplement and replace government

programs that are either being dropped or that fail to provide adequate care for needy individuals. Community, church, and family care systems must be quickly catalyzed to assume a major share of the responsibility in meeting human needs in the eighties and nineties, and the church is in an optimum position to do this. Personally, I am convinced the church can "do it better" if we grasp the opportunity. . . .

In order to work for Christ's Kingdom in the eighties and nineties, however, *the church will have to disavow its mindless support of secular agendas of the left, right, or middle.*[4]

From *The Mustard Seed Conspiracy* by Tom Sine, copyright © 1981; used by permission of Word Books, Publisher, Waco, Texas.

To live as true citizens of the Kingdom of God, committed to the compassionate war against suffering, death, and injustice, we must become authentically liberal, authentically conservative, authentically pro-life. A genuine liberal will show compassionate liberality by being "generous and willing to share" (*see* 1 Timothy 6:18); he will "look after orphans and widows in their distress" (*see* James 1:27). A genuine conservative will conserve the whole truth of God's Word, "test everything. Hold on to the good" (1 Thessalonians 5:21), and be sure that his agenda is based in Scripture, not in secular political ideologies.

The Church may look weak at times, divided at times, even foolish at times—but Christ has promised that His Church cannot be overcome or defeated. We can win the compassionate war if we will cease to be people of the right, the left, or the middle, and begin to think, speak, and act as people of the Kingdom.

Source Notes

1. Tom Sine, *The Mustard Seed Conspiracy* (Waco: Word Books, 1981), pp. 69,70.

2. *Newsweek* (April 1, 1985), p. 51.

3. Henri Nouwen, "The Desert Council to Flee the World," *Sojourners* (June 1980), p. 18.

4. Sine, *Mustard Seed* pp. 57,58 (emphasis added).

Chapter Eight

Know Your Enemy

Baby Killers—or Victims?

Accept one another ... just as
Christ accepted you, in order to
bring praise to God.

Romans 15:7

I grew up in a little town in Iowa. My dad was a minister,
and our home, the manse, was next door to the home of the
garbage collector and his family. The garbage collector's
son was about my age, and we were friends. He worked
hard at his studies and earned good grades. So did I. My
friend's family didn't have much money, so they weren't
able to send him to college. He went instead to a vocational
school where he studied to be a mechanic. My folks weren't
wealthy, but they were able to scrape enough together to
send me to college. This was in the late 1960s, during the
height of the Vietnam War.

During the war, Selective Service drafted young men out
of vocational schools, but not out of college. I had a student
deferment, my friend did not. My friend, the garbage collector's son, was killed in Vietnam.

I can't think about that without a lot of pain, a lot of regret for the loss of my friend. He was a soldier—but he was

also a victim of that war. He was one of 50,000 young men who lost their lives in that war. And there were other victims, the thousands who were maimed and disfigured. Many survived their hitch physically intact, but with deep emotional scars.

Those who came home were often greeted by crowds— not crowds of well-wishers, but crowds of protesters who hurled curses and abuse at them. These young men thought they had gone to war to serve their country, but when they returned they were called names like "murderer" and "baby killer" and "criminal" by people who claimed to have compassion. Many of the victims of that war were children, old people, peasant farmers trying to survive in a war-ravaged land. But some of the victims were soldiers— nineteen-year-old boys from places like Iowa Falls or Muncie or Bowling Green or Yuba City, forced to participate in the most horrible pastime the human mind has ever devised: the wholesale slaughter of other human beings. The war in Vietnam is over now, but its pain still throbs in our nation's soul.

Today, there is another kind of slaughter going on: abortion, the silent, antiseptic slaughter of 1.5 million innocent victims every year. Of all the wars that have been fought in America's history, the war against the unborn has been the costliest. From the American Revolution to the Vietnam War, just over 1,020,000 American men have fallen in combat. That's half a million *less* than the number of American babies aborted *every year*.

There is a civil war raging in America over the tragedy of abortion. Like every war, this one has its victims. Some are obvious victims—the innocent unborn who are subjected to burning saline injection or dismemberment by suction curettage. But there are other victims as well: women who are caught with an unwanted pregnancy. Some are so young they are little more than children themselves. Some are financially or emotionally unprepared to care for a child.

Many face pressure to abort their babies from parents or husbands or boyfriends. They turn to Planned Parenthood or an abortion clinic for help, and very often they are given inadequate counseling. They are told that the fetus growing within them is merely a blob of tissue, they are misled, they are exploited. In short, they are *victims* of abortion.

Many of these victims, in their confusion and desperation, approach the door of an abortion clinic only to be confronted by a cordon of sloganeering, sign-carrying pro-life activists. And these women suddenly find themselves even further victimized, caught in the ideological crossfire of the abortion wars. In addition to the painful choice they must make, they are subjected to cruel jeers and called names like "murderer" and "baby killer" and "criminal" by people who claim to have compassion.

In every war, there are battle lines, opposing sides, and a violent clash between enemies. In this, as in any war, it's vitally important to know who our real enemy is.

Women with crisis pregnancies are exploited and victimized by abortion for a variety of reasons, not the least of which is sheer profit. They are denied the information they need to make an informed choice. They are denied the emotional and financial support they desperately need to make the best decision for their own and their babies' future. Mothers in trouble are not our enemies, any more than the unborn lives they carry within them.

During the Civil War, Confederate General Thomas "Stonewall" Jackson emerged from his tent one night to find two brawling soldiers, surrounded by a cheering, shouting crowd of men. Jackson stood silently, coldly eyeing the fight until one of his officers noticed his presence and shouted, "Attennn-hut!" The fight broke up in an instant.

Jackson stepped forward and pointed northward. "Gentlemen, you all know we go into battle tomorrow morning. I would remind you that the enemy is over there."

And so it is with us. We all too easily forget who our real enemy is.

The Paramount Issue

In religion as in politics, it so
happens that we have less love for
those who believe half our creed than
for those who deny the whole of it.
                    Charles Caleb Colton

Shall I ask the brave soldier,
who fights by my side in the cause
of Mankind, if our creeds agree?
                    Thomas Moore

There is a young evangelical author who has published a number of best-selling books on the abortion issue. In his writing and speaking, he expresses understandable anger over the issue of abortion. Sadly, however, he seems to reserve his most scornful rhetoric for other Christians. Armed with a lexicon of angry epithets, he rashly scathes Christian leaders, institutions, and publications, doing enormous damage to lives and reputations. Though he agrees with these Christians on a majority of issues regarding Christian faith and action, he has chosen to crucify his fellow Christians over trivial points of disagreement. He views as enemies those brothers and sisters he ought to be encouraging and embracing and working alongside.

I'm convinced that not one single human life has ever been saved by this kind of savagery and slander of one Christian toward another, nor has it brought the practice of abortion one day closer to an end. This activist has flatly stated, "The pro-life issue is paramount," end of sentence. To him, there is no more urgent issue facing Christians than the fight against abortion. And I want to be absolutely clear that there *is* an enormous, overriding urgency to the struggle against abortion. But the abortion issue is *not* paramount according to Scripture. That is, the urgency of this issue does not abrogate the truly paramount law of love.

According to Jesus Christ in Mark 12:28–31, our priorities must be (1) loving and glorifying God with all our heart, soul, mind, and strength; and (2) loving others—particularly others in the Body of Christ. Jesus concludes ". . . There is no commandment greater than these" (Mark 12:31). The unmistakable, inescapable command of God that saturates the pages of the Bible is that we are to preserve the unity of the Body of Christ; to unconditionally love and accept our fellow Christians, regardless of our disagreements; to be gentle and patient toward those with whom we differ; to make every effort to do whatever leads to peace and mutually building each other up.[1]

The Bible speaks clearly to the fact that we are to keep peace in the Body of Christ. Proverbs 6:16–19 lists "seven things which are detestable" to the Lord, and included in this list are the detestable sins committed by both abortionists and some opponents of abortion: "hands that shed innocent blood" and "a man who stirs up dissension among brothers." Disparaging other Christians is such a serious sin that Paul, in 1 Corinthians 5:11, includes it along with sexual immorality, covetousness, idolatry, drunkenness, and unethical business practice as cause for severe church discipline.[2]

If we are to be consistently pro-life, we must respect the sanctity of life of the Body of Jesus Christ. Our efforts on behalf of the unborn must be motivated by compassion, not by anger or revenge. To paraphrase Paul in 1 Corinthians 13, we could give up everything we have and surrender ourselves to be put to death for the sake of the unborn, but without Christlike unconditional love, we would accomplish absolutely nothing. It is not enough simply to love the innocent unborn. After all, it's easy to love a helpless little baby; but God calls us to demonstrate love even when it's difficult to love. He calls us to unconditionally love even those who lack understanding, even those who oppose us, even those who are involved in the detestable sin of abortion itself.

Certainly there is a time for anger—anger directed at injustice, not at fellow Christians. Some people say it's not possible to be angry only at a person's actions and not at the person himself. To this notion C.S. Lewis replies, "I used to think this a silly, straw-splitting distinction: how could you hate what a man did and not hate the man? But years later it occurred to me that there was one man to whom I had been doing this all my life—namely myself. . . . In fact the very reason I hated the [sins] was that I loved the man."[3] In our fight against the sin of abortion, we need to learn what it really means to love our neighbors (especially our Christian neighbors) as we love ourselves, loving even when we strongly disagree with their ideas, even when we strongly hate their actions. Our Christian brother or sister is not the enemy.

The late Dr. Francis A. Schaeffer once wrote, "If we stress the love of God without the holiness of God, it turns out only to be compromise. But if we stress the holiness of God without the love of God, we practice something that is hard and lacks beauty. . . . If we show either of these without the other, we exhibit, not the character, but a caricature of God."[4]

Yes, we must speak the truth, but we must speak the truth (as Ephesians 4:15 makes clear) in love. As followers of Jesus Christ, our pro-life effort is an act of love or it is nothing at all, and it doesn't honor God. The Christian is never confronted with the choice to either speak the truth *or* demonstrate love. He is confronted with the command to do both at the same time—always.

Explosions of Anger

> . . . One of Jesus' companions reached for
> his sword, drew it out and struck the
> servant of the high priest, cutting off
> his ear. "Put your sword back in its
> place," Jesus said to him, "for all who
> draw the sword will die by the sword."
> Matthew 26:51,52

On Christmas Day 1984, three explosions rocked Pensacola, Florida. One bomb damaged the Ladies Center, Inc., a facility exclusively devoted to performing abortions. The other two bombs damaged or destroyed the offices of two physicians who had performed abortions as part of their ob/gyn practices. Federal agents quickly arrested four people, two men and two women, who described themselves as born-again Christians and readily confessed to the bombings. At a press conference following her arraignment for violating federal firearms and explosives charges, one of the women said that the bombings were "a gift to Jesus on His birthday."

Nationwide, there were three abortion clinics bombed or torched by arsonists in 1982 and two more in 1983. In 1984, the number of bombings soared to twenty-four, including the three offices bombed in Pensacola, Florida, on Christmas Day. How do Christians respond to this kind of violence in the name of the pro-life movement? Some were openly appalled and immediately denounced the violence. "The bombings are criminal and terroristic," said one Christian spokesman, "and very damaging to the cause of the unborn."

But other Christian leaders voiced approval, even exultation, over the violence. Said one Pensacola minister: "This isn't terrorism. . . . History will prove that the bombers will be the heroes because they stopped the killing of babies."[5] Similarly, a Christian woman who heads a prominent national anti-abortion organization said, "To me, bombing a clinic is less disastrous than killing children. I don't lose any sleep over it. You wouldn't catch me blowing up one because I don't know anything about explosives. If I didn't have responsibilities, I might."[6]

As Christians, we bear the name of the One who said, "Blessed are the peacemakers, for they will be called the children of God." When soldiers came to take Jesus from the garden of Gethsemane, Peter rose to His defense, wielding a sword. But Jesus ordered Peter to put away his sword, and thus Jesus disarmed His Church forevermore.[7] Violent words and violent acts only serve the purposes of the adversary.

It's easy to see how bombings and arson discredit rather than advance the pro-life cause. But what some of us fail to realize is that the same spirit that produced those bombings is being lived out today within the pro-life movement, and indeed within the Church itself. In less dramatic but equally real ways, explosions of anger, explosions of arrogance, and explosions of harsh rhetoric are also bringing discredit to our cause.

Many Christians have a burden to bring an end to the threat of nuclear devastation that threatens our race. They see the arms race as the number one issue facing mankind and the Church. But if an anti-abortion activist happens to encounter an antinuclear activist in the corridor at church, he will likely jab his finger at his Christian brother's NO NUKES! button and say, "I've got news for you! In the past year, a million and a half little kids were murdered by abortionists—and *not one person* died from a hydrogen bomb!"

If this exchange is noticed by another Christian brother whose burden happens to be world hunger, you may hear him say to the anti-abortion activist, "In the last twenty-four hours, while you've been so concerned about all those babies who've never been born, forty thousand children starved to death around the world. Where's your concern for all the children who are dying for the lack of a cup of rice?"

Then comes the evangelism activist, shaking his head in dismay. "All you people want to do is fill empty bellies. What are you doing about filling empty souls? The *real* issue is that three and a half billion people are headed for an eternity without Christ!"

People come into the Church with different gifts, different burdens, different concerns. We all believe our burden is *the* burden that faces the Church. And it is our nature as human beings to judge those who don't share our burden. There will always be tension in the Church. The tensions we experience with other Christians can be destructive tensions or creative tensions; it all depends on our focus.

What is our focus?

Some prominent Christian activists would answer, "Abortion. That's the paramount issue." But I insist that would be a tragic answer.

Our different burdens and concerns for this dying world act upon the Church like a centrifuge. Unless Jesus and Jesus alone is the focal point, the gravitational center of all we say and do, we will all fly apart—and our cause will be doomed. It is Jesus to whom we must be committed, first and always. It is Jesus alone who is paramount, who is before all things, who in everything has supremacy, who is the head of the Church.

Confronted with this truth, most of us would undoubtedly say, "Well, yes, Jesus is my focus, my center, too! I mean, He's the reason I'm so concerned about the issue of ————." (And we fill in the blank with our favorite issue.) Issues can be so seductive. They can easily overpower our relationship to Christ and other Christians. I have to confess this is a continual struggle in my own life.

I have a burden for the lives of the unborn. It's a concern that is probably heightened by the fact that my wife, Shirley, had two difficult pregnancies, and at different times we nearly lost both of our children. I have a burden for the hungry children of the world—a concern deepened by the experience of kneeling in a hunger-ravaged African village and holding malnourished children in my arms. I have a burden for those who are lost without Jesus Christ, because I have richly tasted the joy of knowing Him. And I have a deep burden for the peace of the world, a concern born partly of the pain I felt when a friend of mine was killed in Vietnam.

In different ways, that war brought pain to us all. During those turbulent years, the hearts of many pastors were filled with compassion and a sincere desire to be Christlike peacemakers in a troubled world. So they began to speak out against the Vietnam War. Indeed, in many American churches you knew you were going to hear a sermon calling for peace in Vietnam every Sunday.

But with the end of the war in 1975 came the collapse of the antiwar movement. For those churches that had preached single-mindedly against the war, it was as if they had been pushing and straining against a closed door, only to have it suddenly flung open from the other side. The predictable result is collapse, and many of these churches did collapse and die. Why? Because they had a false center. They were focused on the issue of Vietnam, not on the person of Jesus Christ.

Many Christians run the same risk today: the risk of becoming hollowed out by issues, of becoming ripe for collapse. The issue is no longer war in Vietnam, but a whole new range of challenges posed by a lost and hurting world. *No cause*—even the noble cause of justice for the unborn—is more important than our obedience to Jesus Christ and His law of unconditional love.

War in the Sanctuary of Life

Spiritual warfare is just
as brutal as human warfare.
Jean-Arthur Rimbaud

In *Aborting America*, Bernard Nathanson recalls the pro-abortion movement of the 1960s in which he once played a key role. He quotes his then associate Lawrence Lader as saying, "Every revolution has to have its villain. It doesn't really matter whether it's a king, a dictator, or a tsar, but it has to be *someone*, a person, to rebel against. It's easier for people we want to persuade to see it this way."[8] In other words, the pro-abortionists needed an enemy to rally against in their war against pre-1973 abortion laws. The target they selected was the Catholic hierarchy. "Our movement," he concludes, "persistently tarred all opposition with the brush of the Roman Catholic Church or its hierarchy, stirring up anti-Catholic prejudices."[9]

Though the 1973 *Roe vs. Wade* decision has long since put the pro-abortionists in the driver's seat, the abortion wars are still being fought by both sides with much the same strategy: Pick out your enemy, take aim, and start blasting. The result is a lot of heat, a lot of hurt, a lot of smoke—and hardly any light.

Dr. Nathanson expresses his concern that the sloganeers on both sides "have polarized American reactions into dimly understood but tenaciously held positions. The din that has arisen in our land has already created an atmosphere in which it is difficult, if not impossible, for the individual to see the issues clearly and to reach an understanding free from the taint of the last shibboleth that was screamed in her ear."[10]

Justice is the product of reason mingled with compassion. Tragically, neither side in the white-hot abortion war seems inclined to display much of either. The pro-abortionists are wrong, *dead* wrong, and they present a formidable wall of opposition to our efforts on behalf of unborn life. But we can only hurt the pro-life cause by adopting a course of violent confrontation, sloganeering, and smear tactics.

Women with crisis pregnancies are not the enemy. Our fellow Christians are not the enemy—not even those Christians who call themselves pro-choice. Even the hard-core pro-abortionists themselves are not the enemy.

Who, then, is our enemy in the war against abortion?

I believe the answer is found in Ephesians 6:10–12: "... Be strong in the Lord and in his mighty power. Put on the full armor of God so that you can take your stand against the devil's schemes. For our struggle is not against flesh and blood, but against ... spiritual forces of evil...." "Clearly our opponent is a spiritual adversary that rages against God, the author and giver of life. This adversary has taken the war against God into the most holy sanctuary of human life: a mother's womb.

The fight against abortion, like the fight against hunger, oppression, injustice, and spiritual darkness, is part of our spiritual warfare. And spiritual warfare requires an entirely different kind of arsenal than a war against mere flesh and blood. This war can only be fought with weapons of compassion and truth. When we resort to violent words and violent actions, we cease to be part of the solution; we become part of the problem.

Source Notes

1. *See* Leviticus 19:18; Psalm 133; Matthew 5:44; 22:39; Romans 12:3–8; 14:19; 15:5–7; 1 Corinthians 12,13; Galatians 5:13–26; Ephesians 4:1–17; 5:2; Philippians 2:1–8; Colossians 3:12–15; James 3:13–18; and 1 John 3–5.

2. *See also* Proverbs 10:18; 20:19; Mark 7:22; Romans 1:29,30; 2 Corinthians 12:20; Ephesians 4:31; Colossians 3:8; 1 Timothy 3:11; Titus 2:3; and 1 Peter 2:1.

3. "Christian Behavior," *The Best of C.S. Lewis* (Washington: Canon Press, 1969), pp. 493,494.

4. Francis A. Schaeffer, *The Church Before the Watching World* (Downers Grove, Ill.: InterVarsity Press, 1971), p. 63.

5. *Time* (January 14, 1985), p. 17.

6. *People* (August 5, 1985), p. 83.

7. *See* Matthew 26:51,52; Luke 22:49–51; John 18:10,11.

8. Bernard N. Nathanson with Richard N. Ostling, *Aborting America* (Garden City, N.Y.: Doubleday, 1979), p. 51.

9. Ibid., p. 172.

10. Ibid., p. 166.

Chapter Nine

The Aborted Image

A Cosmic Madness

Some generation of mankind was
eventually bound to face the task of
abolishing war, because civilization was
bound to endow us sooner or later with the
power to destroy ourselves. We happen to
be that generation, though we did not ask for
the honor and do not feel ready for it. There is
nobody wiser who will take the responsibility and
solve this problem for us. We have to do it
ourselves.

Gwynne Dyer
War

It was just moments before 5:30 A.M., and the sun was still below the eastern rim of the desert. In the bunker, someone had tuned a radio to the Voice of America, which was softly playing Tchaikovsky's "Serenade for Strings." In the room were physicists, technicians, and soldiers. A voice at the microphone intoned, "Six. Five. Four." The voice began to quaver. "Three. Two. One." Suddenly the microphone dropped from the man's shaking hands as he cried out, "Zero!"

In one silent instant, the sun appeared in the sky—or so it seemed. The fireball that reared itself up over the Trinity test site in New Mexico was in fact hotter than the surface of the sun. The sight of its sky-splitting fury was followed a few seconds later by the earsplitting sound: a deep, roaring, rolling thunder that seemed to go on and on. In those few moments, the world entered a new age, the nuclear age.

Within the bunker, some people laughed, while others wept. Still others were lost in silent contemplation. The leader of the team of scientists who designed the world's first atomic bomb, a thin and frail-looking man named J. Robert Oppenheimer, looked out toward the pillar of fire he had made and something within his mind spoke these words from the Hindu *Bhagavad-Gita*: "I am become Death, the shatterer of worlds."[1]

Twenty-one days later, on August 6, 1945, the bomb was exploded in anger over a place called Hiroshima, casting a cloud over a ruined city and over the entire future of mankind. Of that day, Oppenheimer would later say, "The physicists have known sin, and this is a knowledge which they cannot use."[2]

But will this knowledge be used? Will there come a day when the terrible bomb again explodes in anger? Will God allow us to destroy ourselves?

I don't know. No one knows.

Some people claim to know the future. They claim to be able to read the Book of Revelation as if it were a road map. I am sorry, but I cannot. Eschatology is not an exact science.

I believe God holds the future, and that He has a plan for the human race. At the same time, I am convinced that God has given human beings free will, and thus He has left a great deal of our own destiny in our hands. Would God allow us to destroy ourselves? Consider this: Would God allow 1.5 million babies to be aborted every year? Would God allow 15 million children to die of starvation every year? Would God allow millions more throughout the world to enter eternity without any knowledge of Himself?

We who ask why God allows such suffering in the world should consider this question: Why do *we* allow it?

I believe God is active and imminent in the world. But I also believe the people of God are called to be active and imminent in the world. As Randy Stonehill sings,

> *We are His hands, we are His voice;*
> *We are the ones who must make the choice.*[3]

Indeed, we are His hands and voice; we are the Body of Christ. We are called to be in the game, not waiting on the sidelines for the final gun to sound.

That gun could go off at any second. There is nothing vaguely conjectural about the plans for global nuclear war. With only a limited amount of flexibility, the entire war has essentially been plotted and programmed into guidance control computers aboard thousands of missiles. The targets are in the computers at this very moment. All that is needed is for someone to push the button.

The Cuban missile crisis of October 1962 brought the world eyeball-to-eyeball with final annihilation. At the height of the tensions, President Kennedy and Premier Khrushchev were engaged in an olympian test of wills. United States bombers circled the outskirts of the Soviet Union like nuclear-armed birds of prey. Those who understood the crisis were terrified. Physicist Leo Szilard, who in 1939 had pressed the United States government to develop the atom bomb, boarded a plane for Switzerland. Even after the crisis was resolved and the missile-laden Soviet ships turned back for home, high military advisors urged the president to launch a preemptive nuclear strike on the U.S.S.R.[4]

Since then, we have approached the same brink again and again—not as closely as in 1962, perhaps, but close enough. The tensile strength of the nuclear trip wire has been put to the test by blinded satellites, computer glitches, and bungled secret submarine maneuvers in hostile waters. On several occasions, military war gamers have flashed simulated launch orders to missile crews who didn't know they were simulated; disaster was averted with only minutes to spare.

We live our day-to-day lives just a whisker from total war. The theory of deterrence (which says war will never occur because both sides know they would surely be destroyed) has begun to crumble. Strategists on both sides are studying plans to "win" a final war. Behind all the talk of "counterforce first strikes," "damage limitation," and "strategic defense initiatives" is the fact that nuclear war is becoming more and more likely with each passing day.

"The superpowers," observes Nigel Calder, "steeped in their own propaganda, have never been adept at seeing the other fellow's point of view."[5] Thus we see a black vs. white, good vs. evil struggle between "capitalist imperialism" on one side and "the evil empire" on the other. Is there truly an evil empire in the struggle between East and West?

Certainly it is not difficult to find evil in an empire that has in its history the stench of Stalinist blood purges, the misery of the Gulag, the invasions of Hungary and Afghanistan, the subjugation of eastern Europe, and the suppression of free speech and free thought from one end of a continent to the other. At the same time, I fear for the soul of that other empire: the empire that seems unwilling to face the nature of its own evil in places like Dresden, Hiroshima, and Vietnam, and which—out of misplaced self-interest and narcissistic arrogance—continues to support oppressive right-wing dictatorships around the world. As John Stott observes, "The East is far from being wholly evil, and the West from being wholly good."[6]

There *is* a truly evil empire that threatens the human race, but that evil empire has no capital in Washington or Moscow. "Our struggle," says the apostle Paul, "is not against flesh and blood, but against the rulers, against the authorities, against the powers of this dark world and against the spiritual forces of evil in the heavenly realms" (Ephesians 6:12). Those heavenly realms are the spiritual domains that overlook this battlefield called Earth. Paul further explains that God has an eternal plan that He is working out through human history—and particularly through the action of His visible Church—whereby "the manifold wisdom of God" is being "made known to the rulers and authorities in the heavenly realms" (*see* Ephesians 3:10).

The forces that are now operating in this dark world and in the heavenly realms—forces that are identified in Scripture with the person of Satan—are at war with God's eternal plan, and they are attacking His creation at many different points. We can only catch fleeting glimpses of this cosmic struggle in the pages of Scripture and the pages of human history. The overall pattern of the war between ultimate good and total evil has not been fully disclosed to us, but a few things are clear.

In His eternal plan, God created human beings to be a reflection of His own perfect character: "So God created man in his own image, ... male and female he created them" (Genesis 1:27). But that image was shattered by sin. The image of God remains in us, but in distorted form, like the reflection in a broken mirror. Romans 8:29 tells us that, in His eternal plan, God determined that we should be *conformed to the image of Christ*. That is, God is restoring His shattered image in us by refashioning us in the likeness of His Son, Jesus Christ.

The satanic plan, however, is to totally eradicate the image of God. The forces of the heavenly realms gained a significant but partial victory over humanity with the introduction of sin to the human race (*see* Genesis 3; Romans 5:12–21). To this end, satanic forces seek to deceive, seduce, and neutralize the Christian Church; to erase the image of God from our view of ourselves (the process of dehumanization); and, if possible, even to erase human life from the world by nuclear holocaust, thereby scouring the last traces of the image of God from the planet.

If we look at human history in light of spiritual warfare, a striking pattern emerges. Racism, exploitation, holy wars, political wars, acts of murder and rape, indifference and apathy, abortion, and the nuclear menace cease to be isolated and disparate aspects of social and individual conduct. All these horrors are cut from the same cloth.

If, for example, the Constitution tells me a black man is only three-fifths human, then the image of God must be partially or totally absent from him, and I am free to make him my slave, my property.

If, as a Christian in the Middle Ages, I believe the image of God resides in me but not in the Muslim infidel, then I can slay him with the sword in a holy war for the cause of Christ.[7]

In order to rape or kill, I must (at least on some unconscious level) come to see my victim as a thing, a depersonalized object fit only to be used and discarded for my own gain or amusement. To depersonalize someone is to discard the image of God within that person.

If black or brown people in another part of the world are dying of hunger we rationalize, "Well, it's sad, of course, but they're so far away. If only they worked harder, like I do, they wouldn't be hungry." The unexamined rationale behind such thinking (which I've found to be common even among Christians) is that the image of God dwells more fully in "us" than in "them."

And, of course, the pro-abortion position presents the purest expression of depersonalization ever conceived. The entire issue centers on the question, "Is the fetus a person?" From a biblical standpoint, this is simply a question of whether or not the unborn bear the image of God. The image of God was stripped from the unborn by judicial fiat in 1973, freeing us to kill human beings while we tell ourselves we are "terminating fetal tissue."

And what of nuclear war? Without question, Satan's final solution to the problem of the image of God would be to simply scorch it from the face of the earth with a nuclear blowtorch. Destroy the people, destroy the image.

As early as 1946, long before the world awoke to the globally destructive potential of nuclear weapons, Albert Einstein warned, "The unleashed power of the atom has changed everything save our mode of thinking, and thus we drift toward unparalleled catastrophe."

Ten years later, in 1956, President Eisenhower expressed this hopeful wish:

> When we get to the point, as we one day will, that both sides know that in any outbreak of general hostilities ... destruction will be both reciprocal and complete, possibly we will have sense enough to meet at the conference table with the understanding that the era of armaments has ended and the human race must conform its actions to this truth or die.[8]

Today it is clear that Eisenhower's hope was forlorn and Einstein's catastrophic fear is just a hair's breadth from realization. Why do we allow ourselves to be used as accomplices in the satanic plan for our own destruction? Why do we recklessly, eagerly continue to build doomsday devices on an endless conveyer belt? Surely, from a reasoned point of view, the arms race must seem a form of racial madness. Indeed, as Nigel Calder observes:

> It is utterly mad, as any visiting alien from another planet would tell you at once, but it is no ordinary psychosis, the work of homicidal maniacs or the crazy scientists of popular imagination. The cosmic madness that threatens to destroy [our] civilization is the product of policies that responsible governments have developed conscientiously and thoughtfully over many years.[9]

Calder is correct in calling the nuclear arms race no ordinary psychosis but rather a cosmic madness—a madness inflicted on mankind by rulers, authorities, and powers in the cosmic realms. It is the same quality of madness exemplified by the $500 million per year abortion industry, an industry which, like the nuclear weapons industry, is the product of deliberate policies of a responsible government.

As Christians, we are called to be peacemakers, willing to lay down our lives to make a creative, pro-life difference in this perilous world. We must be people of faith, willing to believe that through the power of God we can discover the resolve, the wisdom, and the power to reverse the course of the arms race. God's people cannot afford the mood of pessimism and resignation that so many in our world mistake for realism; authentic faith is an optimism rooted in the reality of God's active power.

God calls us to exercise this kind of authentic faith through prayer and pro-peace activism in the world. In 1 Timothy 2:2, we are called to a life-style of committed prayer "for kings and all those in authority, that we may live peaceful and quiet lives in all godliness and holiness." In our private prayers and in our public intercession as we worship together, we should be lifting up prayer to God for the peace of the world, for our own nation, and for those nations that we must sadly, regretfully regard as enemies.

If we claim to be Christian peacemakers according to God's call, then we must live as peacemakers within a community of peace and unconditional love. In his book *Involvement: Being a Responsible Christian in a Non-Christian Society*, John Stott observes:

> God's call to us is not only to "preach peace" and to "make peace" but also to embody it. . . . He means his Church to be a sign of his Kingdom, that is, a model of what human community looks like when it comes under his rule of righteousness and peace. . . . We can hardly call the world to peace while the Church falls short of being the reconciled community God intends it to be. If charity begins at home, so does reconciliation. We need

to banish all malice, anger, and bitterness from both Church and home, and make them instead communities of love, joy, and peace. The influence for peace of communities of peace is inestimable.[10]

Our failure as Christians to become the embodiment of peace in the world is exemplified by our division over the peace issue itself. Clearly the arms race is an issue over which many Christians strongly differ. Presumably, of course, all Christians believe in peace per se. Some, however, believe in peace through disarmament while others believe in peace through military strength. This, of course, is no minor disagreement.

Yet if Christians would just open their hearts, minds, and ears to one another, their stereotypes would be replaced with truth and understanding. They would begin to discover that opponents of the arms race are not really agents of totalitarian evil, nor do pro-militarist Christians fit the image of a war-hungry Dr. Strangelove. Whatever our differences over how to achieve peace, we must unconditionally love and accept one another as we focus together on our common center, Jesus Christ, the Prince of Peace.

Ultimately, however, I believe we in the Church must learn to find our security and peace in Christ alone, not in reliance upon nuclear weapons. Ours must be the faith of the Psalmist, who wrote, "Some trust in chariots and some in horses, but we trust in the name of the Lord our God" (Psalm 20:7). Today the leaders of East and West place their trust in the more than 50,000 nuclear devices in their respective arsenals. But if we stay on our present course, these weapons will almost certainly turn and rend us all. As Gwynne Dyer writes:

Nothing is inevitable until it has actually happened, but the final war is undeniably a possibility, and there is one statistical certainty. Any event that has a definite probability, however small, that does not decrease with time will eventually occur—next year, next decade, next century, but it will come. Including nuclear war.[11]

Leading scientists are now convinced that such a war— even if it involved only a small fraction of our present arsenals—would cause the world to be enveloped in dense clouds of dust and ash, thrown up by the profusion of nuclear blasts. The sun's light would be obscured; the world's temperature would drop by as much as a hundred degrees Fahrenheit. After the fire would come the ice, and the long night of nuclear winter. We now know that total war would not simply mean millions or even billions dead, and human civilization crippled. It would in fact be the end of all things, utterly and finally.

The image of God is an image of love, creative power, and life. The image of Satan is hatred, destruction, and death. It is this second, hellish image that mankind is willfully becoming conformed to. Oppenheimer knew: We have become death, the shatterers of our own world, the immolators of our own children.

We have relaxed our vigilance while our satanic adversary prowls around like a roaring lion, lusting for death and blood, looking for someone to consume. He will destroy us, and the image of God within us, by any means possible. He will destroy us with our own lusts, our own fears, our own hatreds. He will seduce us into killing ourselves with our own machines, and even into killing our own children by the millions.

God calls us to stand firm, to be vigilant, and to resist the adversary at all costs. The destiny of the human race is in the hands of this generation, in your hands and mine.

Justice and Compassion

Does a woman have the right to bear
to full viability an infant whom

she neither wants nor has the capacity
to care for? But does she have the
right to kill that same potentially
holy fetus? Is it not strange that
many pacifists are advocates of
abortion? Or that those who would
seek to deprive others of their choice
to abort on the grounds that life
is sacred are so often those who
champion capital punishment?

M. Scott Peck
People of the Lie

One summer evening in 1984, police officer Arthur Koch answered a call about a disturbance in a Fairfield, California, home. Inside that home was an angry, embittered man in a wheelchair who had lost the use of his legs in Vietnam. As the officer was walking around his car to talk to another policeman the man in the house pointed a gun out the window and fired, hitting Officer Koch in the chest. The policeman died a few hours later in an intensive care unit. He was thirty-four years old, and left a wife and three young children.

The policeman's brother, Russ Koch, is a good friend of mine. Russ has a background in law enforcement, and he and I are in the same house church. We have talked together about our feeling of having each lost a brother to a senseless act of violence. Not long ago, I asked Russ how he felt toward the man who killed his brother and toward the whole issue of crime and punishment. Here is his answer:

I don't believe capital punishment would solve anything. Killing the man who killed my brother won't bring him back. I believe it's wrong to take a life, no matter what the circumstances. The whole matter of life and death should be left up to God.

Capital punishment doesn't deter crime. The man pulling the trigger isn't thinking about the consequences sometime months or years down the road. He's not thinking about the possibility of being executed.

.I believe we have an obligation as a society to see that people who kill once don't kill again. We all need to be protected against people who do these things. But taking the man's life would just be an act of revenge, an eye for an eye. There have been times when I've felt anger toward the man who killed my brother, of course. I've had a long, continuous battle against a real feeling of hatred for what he did to my brother and to all of us who are left to grieve for him. But if you dwell on that anger, it will control your life.

I've made up an album on my brother, with clippings and mementos of his life and even of the tragedy itself—the funeral, the testimonials from people who knew my brother, the different acts of kindness and compassion from churches and the community. And that's where I stop. I don't dwell on hatred toward the gunman. I don't follow the trial. It's not that I mind thinking about the past, about the good times when Art was alive, or even about the sorrow I felt over his death. Some of the memories hurt, and I grieve, and that's to be expected. It hurts to see Art's wife and children struggling to adjust to life without a husband and father. But I refuse to dwell on revenge.

My friend Russ has made a healing choice for this terrible tragedy in his life, a choice to remember without bitterness, to leave matters of life and death with God. He is able to make this choice because he has put his trust in a man who was executed on a hill outside Jerusalem two thousand years ago.

I was raised in a state where the means of capital punishment was the electric chair. In California, where I now live, the method used is cyanide gas. In Utah it is the firing squad. In recent years, some states have sought an accommodation to public squeamishness over gassings, shootings, and electrocutions by administering a lethal injection to their condemned criminals. Capital punishment thus becomes as neat and tidy as having a sick pet put to sleep at the animal shelter. Like abortion, this new form of capital punishment also places physicians in the ethically untenable position of dispensing death.

Two thousand years ago, capital punishment was anything but quick, neat, and tidy. The death Christ died is perhaps the most hideous and excruciating ever devised. He was scourged raw with a leather whip interwoven with shards of metal and bone. He was beaten, cursed, and humiliated. A crown of thorns was embedded into His scalp. He was prodded through the streets of Jerusalem with the weight of His own death instrument pressing down on His bleeding back. Amid the pain, the thirst, the insects, and the taunts of the crowd, Jesus was nailed to the cross, through His hands and feet. The cross was lifted against the sky and dropped into a hole with a bone-dislocating jolt. Then came the long hours of waiting and suffering until death finally came.

All this was done to a completely innocent man.

Some Christians have suggested that the crucifixion of Christ "hallows" the practice of capital punishment. After all, if Christ had not died on the cross, there would be no Good Friday, no resurrection, no salvation. All this is true, yet it is a mystery to me how the state-ordered execution of the most thoroughly innocent man who ever lived can be used as a rationale for executions today. Properly understood, the sacrifice of Christ on the cross was God's testimony to the sanctity of human life. Jesus took the place of all the guilty—including you and me—so that we all might live. He was executed, remember, in the place of a murderer named Barabbas.

Many Christians, in reading the Old Testament, argue that capital punishment is instituted in Scripture, and that's true. In passages such as Exodus 21 and Leviticus 20, the nation of Israel is given a list of statutes and severe penalties designed to preserve Israel as a pure and undefiled society. These days, however, one rarely hears Christians proposing the death penalty for idolatry, consulting fortune-tellers, adultery, incest, cursing one's parents, or any of the other capital crimes listed in such passages.

Christ brought a new way of dealing with human beings and their sin. Because of Christ, we are no longer under the ceremonial and judicial law of Old Testament Israel. According to Hebrews 10, the old law of ceremony and sacrifices was set aside by the sacrifice of Christ, once for all. This does not mean that the moral law of God, the Ten Commandments, has been revoked. As Jesus Himself made clear in Matthew 5:17, He came not to abolish the moral law but to fulfill it.

Many people see the old judicial law as a code of vengeance and retribution for offenses. The Old Testament injunction of "life for life, eye for eye, tooth for tooth" strikes us as harsh and merciless. In reality, however, the Old Testament judicial law was not a *requirement* of vengeance but a *limitation* of vengeance. The natural tendency of man when he is injured is to become filled with rage and hatred and thus to return twice as much evil as he has received. The judicial law ensured that all retribution be fair, consistent, and proportionate to the offense.

The limitations of the law were designed to teach compassion and mercy, not revenge. It is in the spirit of compassion and mercy that God told Israel, "It is mine to avenge; I will repay . . ." (Deuteronomy 32:35), and "Do not seek revenge or bear a grudge against one of your people, but love your neighbor as yourself . . ." (Leviticus 19:18).

Centuries later, when Jesus came to fulfill the law, He didn't reduce, but rather *increased*, its demand on our lives. That is why Jesus said, "You have heard that it was said to the people long ago, 'Do not murder, and anyone who murders will be subject to judgment.' But I tell you that anyone

who is angry with his brother will be subject to judgment
. . ." (Matthew 5:21, 22). In the same way, Jesus increased
the demand for compassion and mercy toward sinners who
in Old Testament times would have been executed.

In John 8:5, the teachers of the law and the Pharisees
brought an adulteress before Jesus and said. "In the Law
Moses commanded us to stone such women. Now what do
you say?"

Jesus did not answer immediately, but stooped down and
wrote in the dust of the ground with His finger. When He
finally spoke, He said, ". . . If any of you is without sin, let
him be the first to throw a stone at her" (John 8:7). In that
moment, Christ instituted a new order. He disarmed the old
judicial law, replacing it with the new covenant of mercy
and grace.

After Jesus had confronted the woman's accusers with
their own sin, they dropped their stones, turned, and went
away. Jesus then turned to the woman and said, ". . . Has no
one condemned you?"

"No one, sir," she said.

"Then neither do I condemn you," Jesus replied. "Go
now and leave your life of sin" (John 8:10, 11). Jesus clearly
was not soft on sin; while offering forgiveness, He demanded repentance and a changed life.

But is that what our criminal justice system is about? Repentance and changed lives?

God is in the business of redeeming and reconciling sinners—all sinners, including those who have transgressed
against the sanctity of human life. I am convinced that the
death penalty is fundamentally opposed to the essential
focus of the Christian gospel, that focus being the redemption and reconciliation of sinners. Death is irrevocable. To
kill a man is to destroy—for all time and for all eternity—
any chance of his repentance, conversion, and redemption.

But even from a strictly secular, utilitarian viewpoint, we
have to concede that the death penalty is an utter failure.

Contrary to its intended purpose, capital punishment does not deter crime. Countries that have abandoned capital punishment, such as France and Canada, have seen no rise in the murder rate; in fact, the murder rate often shows some decline. The penalty of execution seems no more a deterrent to crime than the penalty of cancer is to cigarette smoking.

Murders are usually committed by people under the influence of uncontrollable passion, enormous stress, or the effect of drugs or alcohol—circumstances that tend to eliminate a person's ability to rationally consider the consequences of his actions. Even those who commit premeditated murder usually believe they have planned so well as to prevent themselves from being apprehended and executed.

Moreover, recent studies show that capital punishment may actually contribute to an *increased* incidence in the murder rate, perhaps as a result of the spirit of vengeance and brutality publicized, state-ordered killings communicate to society. The clear message of capital punishment is that killing is a legitimate way to redress grievances.

The history of criminal justice in America is studded with examples of people who have been punished for crimes they didn't commit. Despite the extensive and complicated maze of appeals, reviews, and safeguards in our present system, the execution of the innocent remains a real possibility. Once a person has been executed, there is no way to overturn his sentence.

The way the death penalty is applied in America is so capricious and arbitrary that it hardly deserves to be considered a form of justice at all. Fewer than 1 percent of all murders result in a death sentence for the perpetrator, and of those who are ultimately consigned to death row, a disproportionately large number are either poor, black, mentally handicapped, or emotionally disturbed. Though many affluent, socially advantaged murderers have passed through our courtrooms, they are almost totally absent from death row.

As it is presently structured, our entire criminal justice system basically contradicts God's plan of redemption and reconciliation. We call our prisons "correctional institutions." Are people genuinely corrected in them? Or shouldn't we be honest with ourselves and admit that our prisons are actually dungeons where we can cage up unwanted people until they either rot or explode in mass violence? In *Who Speaks for God?* Chuck Colson writes:

> A very high percentage, some experts say half, of the young people sent to prisons are homosexually assaulted within the first weeks of incarceration. I have talked firsthand with many victims.
>
> Stories like these are so repulsive I can scarcely think about them without feeling outrage. They intensify my conviction to do something with my life to help eliminate these kinds of horrors.
>
> But even more appalling than these dreadful events is the apparent apathy of the public. These stories—and scores more just like them—have all been well reported. Yet there is little evidence of a public rising up in moral indignation, few demands for reform. Why not?[12]

People often respond to such questions with a sneering reference to "bleeding hearts." But shouldn't our hearts bleed? When we look at a man who has raped or killed or stolen, do we erase the image of God from him in our minds? Do we prove our moral superiority over him by killing him?

Chuck Colson points out that tough treatment of prisoners not only fails to reduce the crime rate, but may actually stimulate crime. He writes:

> The truth is, if stiffer sentences stopped crime, we shouldn't have any crime at all. Consider that the average federal sentence in the U.S. increased from 16.5 months in 1945 to 55 months in 1982—a nearly 400 per-

cent jump. The crime rate, however, rose correspondingly.

Our country imprisons more people per capita than
any other nation except the Soviet Union and South
Africa; yet we have the highest crime rate in the world.
If that's law and order, spare us more.[13]

Certainly society needs to be protected from hardened,
violent criminals. One of the principal reasons for the existence of government is to protect its citizens and punish
crime. As the apostle Paul says in Romans 13:2,3, government is established by God to be a terror to those who do
wrong.

Nor am I suggesting that we make excuses for people
who commit crimes. Poverty, bad family life, and an uncar-
ing society can be factors that contribute to antisocial actions, yet the majority of people who come from such
terrible environments do not turn to crime. Nor do these
social factors explain middle- and upper-class white-collar
crime. People do not commit crimes because they are irresistibly driven to it by factors beyond their control, but because they make *choices*. Human beings are not white mice
whose actions are behavioristically determined; people have
free will, and should be held accountable for their choices.

But when a young man has stolen a stereo, is it justice to
sentence him to months of intimidation, degradation, and
homosexual rape? Is it even sensible to confine him in a
cage with murderers, rapists, and vicious gang members?
Shall we send a person convicted of a minor offense to a
graduate school of crime so that he can learn to commit
major offenses in the future? As Colson says, the question is
not *whether* society should punish, but *how* it should punish.

We can continue to punish in ways that destroy people
and multiply the rage and frustration that contributed to the
original crime—or we can find ways of punishing crime that
are redemptive and constructive and benefit both the criminal and his victim.

A government task force recently recommended that $2 billion be allocated for the building of new prisons, yet it seems clear that new prisons don't stop crime. Wouldn't that money be far better spent finding genuinely practical, sensible, and humane solutions to criminal justice issues? Nonviolent criminals could be placed in community-based programs that enable offenders to reconcile with and make restitution to those they have injured, to be trained in new skills, and to work. Wider implementation of victim-offender reconciliation and rehabilitation programs would make room in existing prisons for the truly dangerous criminals who must be kept away from society at all costs.

In Isaiah 1:17, God tells us, "Learn to do right! Seek justice, encourage the oppressed. Defend the cause of the fatherless, plead the case of the widow." God demands justice, but He also demands compassion. Justice without compassion is not justice at all.

The Judgment Against Sodom

> Every patient in my ward has AIDS,
> and every one of them is dying.
> I don't think even one of them knows
> Christ. The only God they ever hear
> about is the one who's going to
> send all homosexuals to hell. You
> should see the light come on in
> some of those faces when I tell
> them about the God I know—the
> God of love and forgiveness.
>
> Gary, an AIDS victim

My friend Gary faced death with courage and a strong faith in Jesus Christ. Through a long battle with a terminal illness, Gary endured suffering, the loss of many of his friends, and the accusation and condemnation of insensitive

Christians. He died of a disease called AIDS, acquired immune deficiency syndrome.

Gary had a past history of homosexual behavior, but he had recommitted his life to Christ, forsaken his homosexual life-style, and married a Christian young woman who offered him her acceptance and understanding. But by this time, Gary had already been infected with AIDS.

Soon after Gary learned he had AIDS, I asked him, "You're a young man. You have a lot of plans. How do you feel about having AIDS? How does this make you feel toward God?" Amazingly Gary expressed neither anger nor fear toward God. He didn't feel God was vengefully punishing him for his past sins. Rather, he viewed AIDS simply as something he had to fight with God's help. He knew he had sinned, but he also knew he was loved and forgiven by God. When Gary's body finally succumbed to the ravages of AIDS in the spring of 1985, his spirit remained unconquered, for Gary had a deep relationship with Jesus Christ.

The world desperately needs Christians who are willing to care about people with AIDS. The next few years will bring the evangelical church face-to-face with the AIDS epidemic, and Christians must begin to decide how they will respond. There are many Christians with homosexual activity in their past, and many more are locked in a seesaw struggle against homosexual feelings. In recent years, I have personally counseled dozens of Christians, both men and women, who struggle with their sexual identity. Since AIDS can take years to present symptoms after the initial exposure, there is no question that churches will increasingly be confronted with the AIDS epidemic. Will we meet this challenge with Christlike compassion or with contempt?

A biblically Christian attitude towards homosexuality recognizes the difference between homosexual tendencies and the sin of homosexual behavior. Christian compassion calls all people to repentance within an atmosphere of acceptance and forgiveness. It saddens me to see the response of so many Christians to the tragedy of homosexuality and AIDS: stereotyping, name-calling, and off-color jokes. I believe many of us will one day have to answer for the sin of homophobia, that irrational fear, contempt, and even hatred of homosexual people that is so common in the Church today. Do we pray for people who struggle with their sexual identity, or do we label them and write them off? Aren't they also made in the image of God?

Some people say that AIDS is God's judgment on the sin of homosexuality, a plague of God's vengeance, just like the fire that fell on Sodom. But I'm convinced that AIDS is a virus, not a vengeance. Today, about 73 percent of all AIDS cases occur among the homosexual population. That means that over a quarter of all AIDS victims are nonhomosexuals; for what sin is God judging that 27 percent?

And what about the judgment that fell on Sodom? People generally assume that the reason Sodom was destroyed was because of the rampant sin of homosexuality, so much so that the name of the city was actually given to the homosexual act, sodomy. Yet Ezekiel 16:49, 50 tells us, "Now this was the sin of your sister Sodom: She and her daughters were arrogant, overfed and unconcerned; they did not help the poor and needy. They were haughty and did detestable things before me. Therefore I did away with them as you have seen."

Clearly, the judgment against Sodom leaves no room for any of us to feel morally superior to the person who is caught in the sin of homosexuality. Can we honestly say we are not arrogant? Not overfed? Not unconcerned? Have we really stretched out hands of compassion to the poor and needy? Who among us is morally qualified to cast the first stone at an AIDS sufferer?

The Christian gospel is the good news of God's forgiveness and unconditional love. We all have sinned, we all fall short, and it's only by God's grace that so few of us have to pay for our sins with our lives, as my friend Gary did. I believe it's our task as followers of Christ to look at all people, including homosexual people, through the lens of Christian grace and forgiveness. Today we have an unparalleled opportunity to penetrate the homosexual community with the message of new life in Christ.

If we meet this challenge with indifference and self-righteous arrogance, then does not the judgment of Sodom deserve to be *our* judgment as well?

Source Notes

1. Peter Goodchild, *J. Robert Oppenheimer: "Shatterer of Worlds"* (London: British Broadcasting Corporation, 1980), p. 162.

2. Ibid., p. 174.

3. Randy Stonehill, "Save the Children," Word Music, Inc.

4. Nigel Calder, *Nuclear Nightmares* (New York: The Viking Press, 1979), pp. 91, 92.

5. Ibid., p. 132.

6. John Stott, *Involvement: Being a Responsible Christian in a Non-Christian Society* (Old Tappan, N.J.: Fleming H. Revell Co., 1985), 1:135.

7. This, in fact, was the mentality that produced the Crusades of the eleventh, twelfth, and thirteenth centuries—genocidal programs carried out under the banner of the cross of Christ. To this day, the Muslim image of Christianity is one of murderous hatred toward the Muslim people and culture. It is no wonder that these people remain the least receptive of all the world's peoples to the Christian gospel. Sadly, the "Crusades mentality" of previous centuries is alive and well in Christendom today, hindering our willingness to meet the challenge of evangelizing the Muslim world. We prefer to ridicule Muslim culture in stereotypical images of gun-toting fanatics, crazed ayatollahs, and desert sheiks than come to grips with the fact that there are millions of needy people in the Muslim world, made in the image of God, who are hungry for the good news of Jesus Christ.

8. George B. Kauffman, "Hiroshima, Nagasaki and Lessons to Learn," *The Fresno Bee* (August 4, 1985), p. G4.

9. Calder, *Nuclear Nightmares*, p. 8.

10. Stott, *Involvement*, 1:145–146.

11. Gwynne Dyer, *War* (New York: Crown Publishers, Inc., 1985), p. xi.

12. Charles Colson, *Who Speaks for God?* (Westchester, Ill.: Crossway Books, 1985), pp. 81, 82.

13. Ibid., p. 99.

Chapter Ten

No Other Plan

A Message of Tears

The New Testament pattern of evangelism
is a blend of proclamation and
practical meeting of needs. The
hungry were fed, the sick ministered
to, the naked clothed, and the
widows and fatherless cared for.
The music of the believers' selfless
actions became the platform for the
words of the gospel. . . . It is divine
music when believers apply what
they profess to the hurts, pains,
and sorrows of mankind.

Joseph C. Aldrich
Life-Style Evangelism

Tracy was seven years old, growing up in a slum in the
middle of Minneapolis. I got to know her through a ministry of our church that took inner-city children out into the
country for a week of camping and Christian fellowship.
One night after a time of singing, sharing, and laughing
around the campfire, I was walking Tracy back to her dorm
room in the woods. As we were walking, I asked, "Tracy, if
you could have just one wish, what would it be?"

She stopped and looked up at me, this frail little wisp of a child with big, beautiful, expressive eyes, and she said, "Ron, I guess if I had one wish, it would be that I could get hurt—not *too* bad, but just enough to go to the hospital, like in a car crash. Because my friends tell me that in the hospital they give people food every day."

I have thought often of those words of my little friend Tracy, and I have wept for her. I have wept for the little children I held in Africa, many of whom I know are not alive today. In different places around the world today, 40,000 children died of starvation. I believe that to be a Christian is to have your heart broken over the things that break the heart of God. The Bible teaches us that starving, suffering children truly break the heart of God.

I have a friend whose heart is broken over the things that break the heart of God. His name is Bob Osborne. In the past few years, Bob has traveled to Africa and India to see firsthand the human tragedy and quiet devastation of famine, disease, poverty, and ignorance. He doesn't consider himself a professional missionary by any means. He's just an ordinary Christian in an average American church with an extraordinarily large heart for suffering people.

On one trip to India, Bob took as many extra pairs of shoes as he could carry in his luggage. Shoes are a rare commodity in India, and he was planning to leave as many pairs as he could with a community of poor Indian Christians. When he boarded the plane to return to the United States, he was barefoot. After seeing the need of those people, he couldn't help but take the shoes off his own feet and give them to a poor Indian farmer to wear.

At another time, Bob and I were in Africa with a group of pastors and laymen from California. After visiting some extremely devastated and parched regions of Africa, we returned to the World Vision office at Nairobi, Kenya. There I was scheduled to speak to the office staff. Before I got up to speak, I asked each of my traveling companions to say a personal word about what they had seen.

Finally it was Bob's turn to speak. He stepped up to the microphone while a roomful of Christian brothers and sisters, black and white, waited to hear his witness. I could tell that Bob's mind, like mine, was filled with images of sick and suffering men, women, and children. Bob began to give his message. It was a message of tears. He stood before this assembly of fellow Christians totally unable to speak. All he could do was weep.

Then the black brother who was the staff director of the Nairobi office stood and said, "Brother Bob, we understand the message of your tears. We know what you're trying to say to us through your weeping."

Bob Osborne's heart is broken over the things that break the heart of God. I often wonder, "Is mine?"

Is yours?

Christianity began in Jerusalem as a community. It moved to Rome, where it became an institution. It moved to Greece, where it became a philosophy. It moved to Europe, where it became a culture. Then it moved to America where, by the 1980s, it has become little more than a self-fulfillment movement. We hear a lot today about the gospel of possibility thinking, about what God can do for *us*. But do we believe in the possibility of daring great things for God, the possibility of spending ourselves in service to God, the possibility of challenging the evils of hunger, poverty, and spiritual darkness in our world?

In a little African church about an hour outside of Ouagadougou, the capital of Burkina Faso, several other American Christians and I worshiped with a congregation of black brothers and sisters. Despite the poverty and hunger that plagued this parched region of western Africa, the joy and enthusiasm of these believers was evident in the upbeat, praise-filled, drum-accompanied singing. A fellow pastor from my community and I both preached to the assembly as the church's pastor, Sammy Yamaego, interpreted.

Toward the end of the service, the church received the tithes and offerings from the congregation. Two baskets were placed at the front of the little wood-frame sanctuary, one basket for tithes (10 percent of the family's income) and the other for offerings given *above* the tithe. Row by row, these Christians would rise and file to the front of the church to place their gifts in the baskets. The gifts that went in the offering basket went to help meet the needs of other Christian brothers and sisters who were facing starvation. I was deeply moved by the example of these friends who gave sacrificially for the benefit of others, even though in abject poverty themselves.

By contrast, the typical American Protestant is so challenged by the needs of a dying world that he gives an average of twenty-four cents a day through his church to meet those needs. By the standards of those brothers and sisters in Burkina Faso, you and I are fabulously wealthy. But are we known for our compassionate generosity—or for our conspicuous consumption?

We fill ourselves with biblical knowledge, taking pages of notes in church and Sunday school, attending Christian seminars and conferences and camps, but do we ever *exercise* all that knowledge in service to the lost, the neglected and the forgotten in our own communities and in the world? Have we forgotten what it means to be suffering, sacrificing servants for Jesus Christ in a dying world?

A few years ago, I attended a pastors' conference at which Tony Campolo was the featured speaker. He shared the story of a trip he had taken to the Caribbean island of Haiti, the poorest nation in the western hemisphere. He was flown in a small plane to a remote part of the country where hunger and suffering were particularly acute. There, for seven days, he witnessed and assisted the relief work being done by an overworked, undersupplied team of Christian missionaries. The human tragedy he saw there—children sick and dying for lack of a cup of milk, their parents' spirits broken by despair—left him shaken and deeply saddened.

As he was returning to the airstrip for the return trip home, Campolo was accosted by a thin, ill-clad Haitian woman. In her arms was a listless, malnourished infant. "Please," she said tearfully, "take my baby with you."

"I'm sorry," he told her. "I wish I could help you, but I can't take your baby. That would be against the law."

"But my baby will die if he stays here," the mother pleaded. "Please take him with you."

"I'm really sorry," Campolo said, climbing into the plane. "There's absolutely nothing I can do."

The woman continued to plead with him as the door slammed shut and the pilot started the engines. While the plane began to taxi down the grassy airstrip, Campolo looked out the window. The woman stood at the edge of the strip, her baby raised up in her outstretched arms, her lips still moving in a heartbreaking plea Campolo could understand but no longer hear.

As the plane lifted up into the sky, Campolo turned to the pilot and said, "I know the name of that child."

"How do you know the child's name?" asked the pilot.

"The name of that child is Jesus," Campolo replied, "because whatever we do for a child like him, we do for Jesus."

God did not give us spiritual and material gifts to spend on ourselves. He intended us to give those gifts away—and indeed to give *ourselves* away—to the poor, the oppressed, the defenseless. For these are in fact the literal representatives of the Lord Jesus Christ to you and to me. Whatever we do for the least of these, we do for Jesus Christ Himself (*see* Matthew 25:40; John 12:8).

Clearly we are materially rich, but I often wonder how rich are we in spirit? I believe an accurate indication of how spiritually rich we are is in our generosity with our material goods. Yet our giving should not be motivated by guilt. It is not a sin to have been born into a time and place where our material needs are so richly met. God has abundantly blessed us at this time in America, and what God wants is not our guilt but our gratitude, plus our faithful, generous, compassionate response to the many deep needs all around us. God wants our gratitude to be expressed in sharing.

A few years ago I was preaching through an interpreter to a congregation of Masai tribespeople in Kenya. There were 600 Masai Christians packed into a little mud-walled church building designed to hold 200. Some were crowded into the rough wooden pews, some were sitting in the aisles, some were standing along the walls. They had been waiting in that place for two hours for us to arrive by Jeep.

As I preached, the only distraction was the constant coughing, hacking, and sneezing throughout the assembly, for most of these people were very sick. In the last three days before I arrived, ten children of that congregation had died. By the end of that year, two out of every five children in that village would perish because of malnutrition, pneumonia, measles, or some other illness which is easily treated in America.

Death stalked this Masai village. The Masai are hard-working, courageous, industrious people. But what do you do when the ground is parched and cracked, and it will not grow food?

After my message there was a time for the sharing of testimonies and prayer requests. As I listened, I felt I was not only on another continent, but in another era, another period of Christian history. Certainly the first-century Church must have been a lot like this. In this village, Christians met together not only on Sunday mornings, but in small groups during the week in their simple dwellings. Despite the suffering they endured, there was a strong sense of the power of the Holy Spirit moving among the Masai Christians. Scores of people were coming to Christ every week, and there was an overflowing of praise and supernatural joy in that place, even amid all the suffering, grief, and death.

As the time of prayer and sharing began, I was amazed to see that the prayers these Masai Christians were lifting up were essentially prayers of gratitude and praise. To me, these people seemed completely destitute—and yet they were *grateful* to God.

One little boy was thankful to God because he had received a cup of goat's milk every day for a week. It wasn't much, but it was the only nourishment he was receiving, and it kept him alive. *Gratitude.*

One woman was thankful that someone had shared the gospel with her. She had received Christ as her Savior and Lord that week, and she was thankful to God. *Gratitude.*

One young man stood and offered thanks to God for some Bibles that had arrived in the village that week. There were not nearly enough Bibles for everyone, so they carefully tore the book into sections. One family was given the Gospel of John, another the Book of Isaiah, another the Book of Acts, and when they finished reading these, they would trade them to another family for a different book. *Gratitude.*

One young mother was thankful to God that some American Christians had sponsored her child through World Vision. Now she knew her child would be alive for another year. *Gratitude.*

Throughout the week we spent in that village, I was struck by the pervasive spirit of gratitude I saw there. Jim Patterson, Bob Osborne, and the others on our team were also moved by the attitude of these people. In the midst of drought, disease, starvation, and death: *gratitude.* Our Masai brothers and sisters in Kenya are physically poor, but spiritually wealthy.

You and I are rich in the things of this world. But could it be that we are spiritually destitute?

In the Sermon on the Mount, Jesus said we are the light of

the world, and I believe one of the primary ways we penetrate the world with the light of God's love is by our generosity and our involvement in the suffering of others. Isaiah
58:10 says, "And if you spend yourselves in behalf of the
hungry and satisfy the needs of the oppressed, then your
light will rise in the darkness, and your night will become
like the noonday."

True wealth of the spirit is rooted in gratitude. True gratitude is expressed in sharing, in spending ourselves in behalf
of the hungry, the sick, and the oppressed. So may our light
shine in a world of death and darkness.

Becoming Pro Eternal Life

> The great tragedy of modern evangelism
> is in calling many to belief but
> few to obedience. The failure has
> come in separating belief from
> obedience, which renders the gospel
> message confusing and strips the
> evangelistic proclamation of its
> power and authority. The evangelistic
> question has become what do we
> believe *about* Christ rather than
> are we willing to forsake all and
> follow him. When the theology of
> faith is torn apart from the life
> of faith, what results is an evangelism
> that has more to do with doctrine
> than with transformation.
>
> Jim Wallis
> *Agenda for Biblical People*

In his book *Life-Style Evangelism*, my friend Joe Aldrich re-
counts a legend about the day Jesus ascended into heaven
following His resurrection. According to this legend, Jesus
was approaching His throne, still bearing the marks of the

nails in His hands and feet and the wound in His side. The angel Gabriel came to Him and said, "Master, You must have suffered a terrible wound while on earth."

"Yes, I did," replied Jesus.

And Gabriel asked, "Do all the people in the world know what You did, the pain You suffered, and the love You showed them?"

"No," said Jesus. "No, not yet. For right now, only a handful of people in Palestine know."

"Then how will the world ever come to know about You and Your love?"

"I have commanded Peter, James, and John," said Jesus, "and a few more of My friends to tell other people about Me. Those who are told will tell still others, and My story will continue to spread to the ends of the earth. Ultimately, all people will know of Me and My love for them."

But Gabriel, knowing the nature of man, was skeptical. "What if Peter, James, and John grow weary? And what if the people who come after them grow indifferent about telling their neighbors about You? Then what? What other plan do You have?"

And Jesus replied simply, "I have no other plan."[1]

Twenty centuries later, He still has no other plan.

I believe we are called to a life-style that is uncompromisingly pro-life. We are not free to pick and choose between issues affecting life. We are not free to say, "Unborn life is made in the image of God, but the lives of convicts, the lives of the poor, and the lives of the neglected are not worth my time." All human life is a gift from God, and must be cherished. Most of all, I believe we are called to a life-style that is pro eternal life. The eternal life of human beings is the most precious gift of all.

The Christian gospel walks on two legs. One leg is the truth of the death and resurrection of Jesus Christ; when we commit ourselves to Jesus Christ as the Lord of our lives, we receive a quality of life that never ends. The other leg of the gospel is the demand of the gospel upon our lives—the demand that we love and show compassion to a suffering world, that we seek justice for the poor and oppressed and defenseless. If our gospel only has one leg or the other, it is crippled and has no power.

The two-legged gospel calls us to become consistently, committedly pro-life—working to end the legalized crime of abortion, working to reform the prison environment, working to end the threat of nuclear devastation, working to end hunger. The two-legged gospel calls us to be pro eternal life—willing to share the good news of Jesus Christ with others around us and throughout our world, at every opportunity, by every possible means.

Let me pose an analogy: There is a word that brings a very bitter taste to my mouth: cancer. I have come to intensely detest that word because of the pain and death it has caused so many of my closest friends and family members. Today there is still no cure for many forms of cancer. Research scientists are working virtually day and night in search of a cure for this disease. I believe the cure will one day be found. When that cure has been discovered and tested and is ready to be used, it will be entrusted to qualified physicians who are appointed to dispense it.

Now, it would be difficult to think of anything more tragic than to have in my own hands the cure for cancer and to keep it to myself. If I really care about the sanctity and the quality of human life, if I am truly pro-life, then I will want to aggressively share the news of this amazing cure with all those who suffer with the disease.

Mankind is sick with the cancer of his alienation and separation from God, and God has entrusted you and me with the cure for this cancer. Will we share the good news of God's solution to the human crisis? Will we love enough to share with others how we have been cured of the cancer of sin and brokenness in our own lives? Or do we really love others so little that we choose to willingly leave them in a place of separation—*eternal* separation—from God?

Are we truly pro-life or are we just anti-abortion? Do we care as much for the lives and souls of men and women around us, in our neighborhoods, our work places, our prisons and jails, our hospitals, our world, as we care for those lives that haven't been born yet? That, in truth, is what it *really* means to be pro-life.

People are suffering and dying in sin and alienation today. You and I can reach them. We *must* reach them, for we are the ones God has chosen to make the crucial pro-life difference in our generation.

And God has no other plan.

Source Notes

1. Joseph C. Aldrich, *Life-Style Evangelism* (Portland: Multnomah Press, 1981), pp. 136–137.

Index